The Bach Cello Suite No. 2 Study Book

by Cassia Harvey

CHP454
©2026 C. Harvey Publications®
All Rights Reserved.
www.charveypublications.com - print books & free sheet music blog
www.learnstrings.com - downloadable books & chamber music

The Bach Cello Suite No. 2 Study Book
Table of Contents

Prelude	Page
Part One (measures 1-4)	2
Part Two (meas. 5-8)	7
Part Three (meas. 9-12)	10
Part Four (meas. 13-20)	16
Part Five (meas. 21-29)	22
Part Six (meas. 30-35)	29
Part Seven (meas. 36-39)	34
Part Eight (meas. 40-48)	37
Part Nine (meas. 49-54)	42
Part Ten (meas. 55-63)	46

Allemande	Page
Part One (meas. 1-4)	52
Part Two (meas. 5-8)	56
Part Three (meas. 9-12)	59
Part Four (meas. 13-16)	63
Part Five (meas. 17-20)	66
Part Six (meas. 21-24)	69

Courante	Page
Part One (meas. 1-6)	72
Part Two (meas. 7-12)	75
Part Three (meas. 13-16)	77
Part Four (meas. 17-22)	80
Part Five (meas. 23-28)	83
Part Six (meas. 29-32)	86

Sarabande	Page
Part One (meas. 1-6)	88
Part Two (meas. 7-12)	90
Part Three (meas. 13-20)	93
Part Four (meas. 21-28)	98

Menuet I	Page
Part One (meas. 1-8)	102
Part Two (meas. 9-18)	108
Part Three (meas. 19-24)	111

Menuet II	Page
Part One (meas. 1-8)	114
Part Two (meas. 9-14)	116
Part Three (meas. 15-24)	118

Gigue	Page
Part One (meas. 1-8)	121
Part Two (meas. 9-14)	124
Part Three (meas. 15-24)	126
Part Four (meas. 25-32)	130
Part Five (meas. 33-40)	132
Part Six (meas. 41-48)	134
Part Seven (meas. 49-60)	138
Part Eight (meas. 61-76)	141

Complete Suite	Page
Prelude	146
Allemande	148
Courante	150
Sarabande	152
Menuet I	153
Menuet II	153
Gigue	154

About this Book

This book divides the second Solo Cello Suite by J. S. Bach into short sections and provides exercises for mastering each section.

The exercises are written to benefit both the professional and the student.

Each exercise was written to teach a specific skill. **Shifts** are often repeated to help with acquiring muscle memory. **Double stops** are included for establishing relative pitch, building left-hand strength, and balancing the bow across two strings. **Intonation** is a main focus of the book, as much of the challenge in playing Bach's Second Suite is playing in tune.

Bach's Suites are not mere etudes as many cellists once thought. They are hauntingly beautiful works that demand our very best technique and deserve our deepest, strongest interpretation.

Many teachers teach the Bach Suites by passing on their own interpretation. I discovered the Suites on my own at nine years of age, unbeknownst to my teacher, who thought that children should not be allowed to play Bach. Subsequent teachers, in disallowing my interpretation and insisting on their own, caused me to dislike the Suites themselves and avoid playing them for over 20 years. I have come to realize that our interpretations of Bach are highly personal and necessarily unique. When teachers pass on to their students their ideas about interpretation, they should be careful not to present them as rules. I have found that the best approach is to help students arrive at their own interpretation.

This book attempts to help cellists competently play the Suite so that they can add their own interpretation. Bach's music can be played by cellists of all levels as soon as they know enough of the notes and positions required to play through the music. There is no room for snobbery or exclusion in teaching the Bach Cello Suites or any other music. We are all trying to play to the best of our ability, and with any genuine effort we will manage to get a good glimpse of Bach, who himself gave us a good glimpse of heaven.

Before these bowings and fingerings were chosen, numerous editions, including the available manuscripts were studied. This edition began with an urtext approach, but adds some commonly accepted bowings and fingerings where they may be helpful, with the hope of producing a kind of *urtext plus common-sense* result.

-Cassia Harvey

Notes on Technique

Bowings

Bowings in the excerpts were chosen to reflect manuscript sources while still being practical. However, bowings are very personal and may be changed to suit the individual player. If the bowings in an excerpt are changed, the bowings in the accompanying exercises should also be changed.

Fingerings

Fingerings were chosen to reflect common practice, bringing together ideas from multiple editions and performance sources. Fingerings are also very personal. When fingerings are changed in an excerpt, the fingerings in the accompanying exercises should also be changed.

Alternate fingerings are occasionally presented below the notes. In this case, exercises were written for the more difficult of the two fingerings. This does not mean that the more difficult fingering is recommended; simply that it needs more support.

Tempo Markings

Many of the exercises were written to be slower than the Suite so that the piece can be learned methodically and carefully. However, once learned, exercises can be played with increasing physical speed, eventually reaching the performance tempo.

Metronome markings are included to give very general guidelines. Metronome markings for the Suite movements were chosen to reflect common performance tempos of today. However, cellists should ultimately choose the tempo for each movement based on their own interpretation.

Extended, Closed, and Contracted Positions

The term *extend* (**Ext.**) as used in the exercises refers to an extended or stretched hand position. The traditional method of extending is to reach a whole step with first and second fingers so that the hand can span two whole steps. *When extending, it is extremely important to move the thumb up under 2nd finger.* The term *closed* (**Cl.**) refers to the typical cello hand position that spans one whole step and one half step. In this book, *closed* is often used to remind the cellist to stop extending.

In this book, the term *contract* refers to an unnaturally closed hand position. To *contract,* pick the fingers between the two contracting fingers up in the air. Move the two contracting fingers close enough to play the second note without lifting the original (or lower) finger off of the cello.

Vibrato

Vibrato (**Vib.**) is used in the exercises to help build hand balance, flexibility, and strength, and to prepare the hand to use vibrato in performance. If you wish to perform the Suite without vibrato, feel free to disregard this direction.

©2026 C. Harvey Publications® All Rights Reserved.

Strings

Strings are indicated by Roman numerals under the notes:

I = A string, II = D string, III = G string, IV = C string

Trills

In this book, trills are played by starting on the note above the written note (the note above the written note is the note you are trilling *to*). Fingerings for trills are thus written (for instance) 2-1, indicating that cellists should start the 1-2 trill with 2nd finger. As this is part of the interpretation, this is optional.

Double Stops

Double stops in the exercises may be omitted by cellists with very small hands but should otherwise be played. In this book, double stops are used to build strength and muscle memory and are crucial for improving intonation.

Dynamics

Cellists often choose to use dynamics that follow the phrase or sentence of music. When the notes go up scale-wise, a crescendo can be played. When the notes go down, a decrescendo can be played. However, this is only a starting point. There are a number of cases (for example, measure 4 of Menuet I) where a crescendo could work well as the phrase goes down. As you play, pencil in dynamics that make sense to you and then keep them if they stand the test of repeated playing.

Some notes are more important than others. Once you have learned the technique of the Suite, you can spend a lifetime deciding which notes to elevate above others and thus avoid playing in a monotone. Traditionally, these elevated or favored notes are played after a crescendo to make their importance more believable.

How to Practice this Book

- Use the exercises to help you master each excerpt.
- Play exercises slowly at first and then build up to the actual tempo of the excerpt.
- Use vibrato on the exercises once the notes are learned and in tune.
- Metronome markings for exercises are only suggestions! Feel free to play the exercises slower or faster to suit your needs.
- When you have finished the exercises in a section, return to the excerpt to play it and see your progress.
- The entire Suite is at the back of the book.
- Play-Along Tracks and other companion materials are available for purchase on the Resource Hub page: www.learnstrings.com/pages/bach2resourcehub

Resource Hub Page

©2026 C. Harvey Publications® All Rights Reserved.

The Bach Cello Suite No. 2 Study Book

Suite by J.S. Bach
Exercises by Cassia Harvey

1. *Prelude, Part One*: Measures 1-4

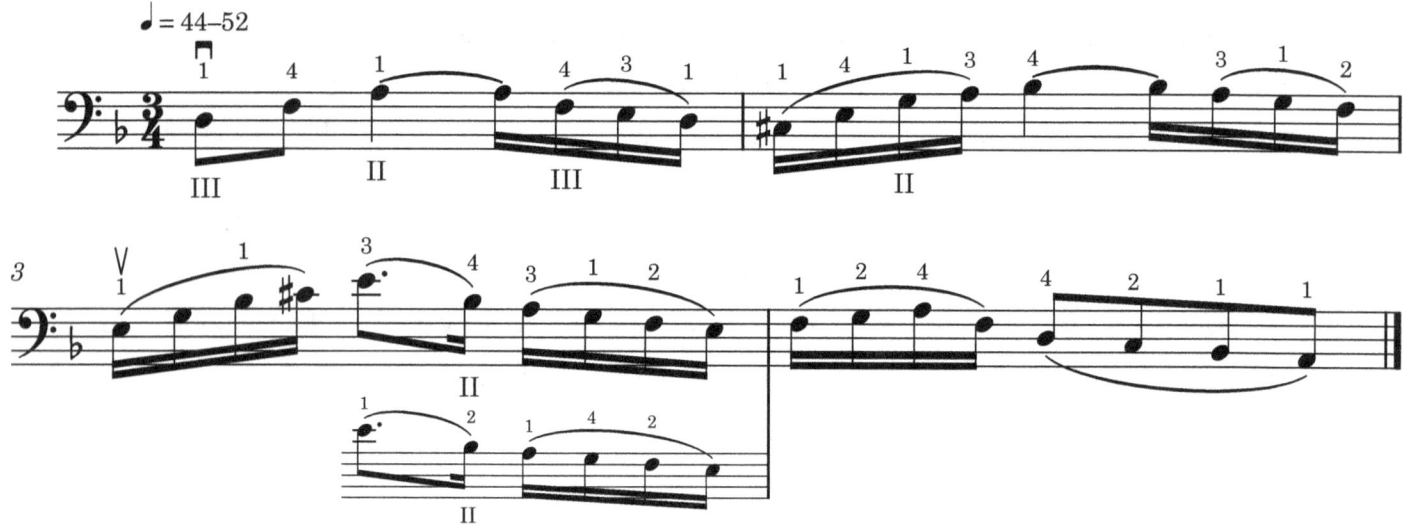

2. Learning the Notes in Fourth Position: Measure 1

3. Agility and Intonation in Fourth Position: Measure 1

©2026 C. Harvey Publications® All Rights Reserved.

The Bach Cello Suite No. 2 Study Book - Prelude

4. Intonation Across Strings in Fourth Position: Measure 1

5. Shifting Back 1/2 Step: Measures 1-2

6. Extending Back to C♮: Measures 1-2

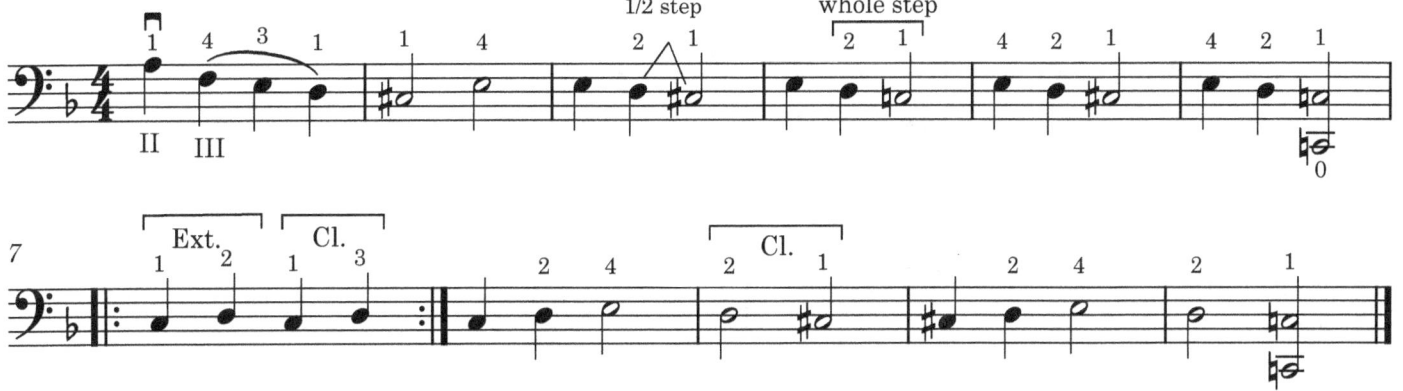

©2026 C. Harvey Publications® All Rights Reserved.

7. Reaching Back Across Strings: Measures 1-2

8. Learning the Notes in Third Position: Measures 1-2

9. Shifting With Agility: Measures 1-2

The Bach Cello Suite No. 2 Study Book - Prelude

10. Rhythm: Measures 1-2

11. Intonation: Measure 3

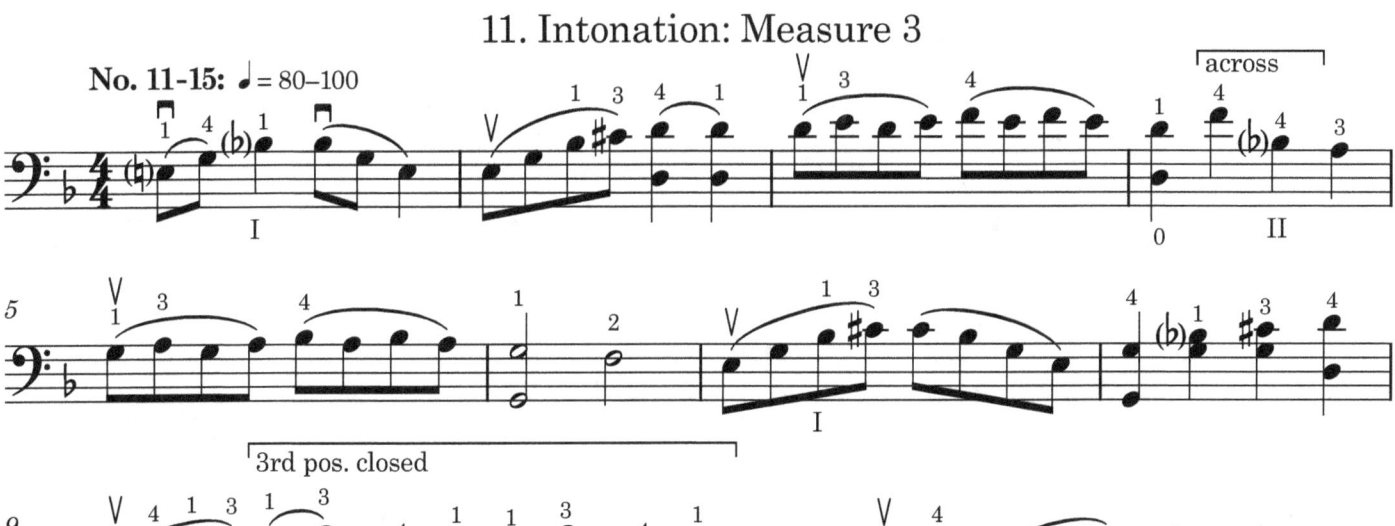

12. Shifting: Measure 3

©2026 C. Harvey Publications® All Rights Reserved.

The Bach Cello Suite No. 2 Study Book - Prelude

16. *Prelude, Part Two*: Measures 5-8

17. Intonation: Measure 5

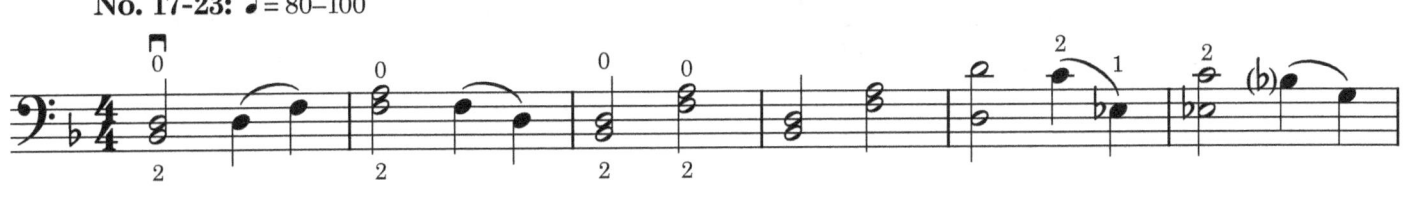

18. Extensions Across Strings: Measure 6

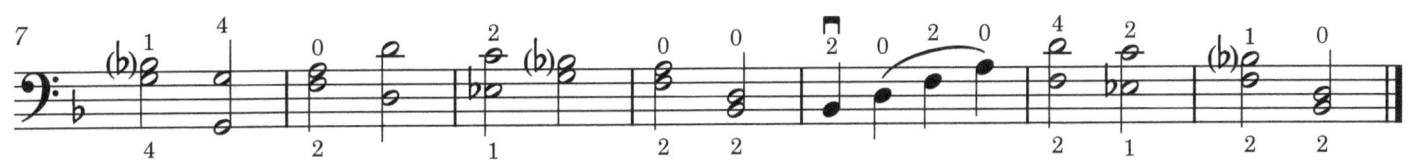

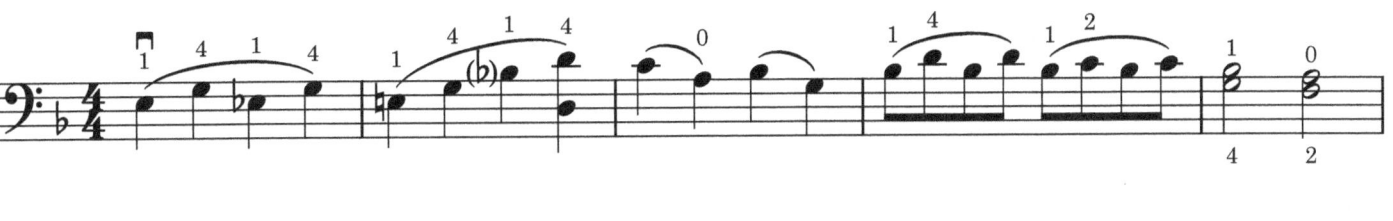

19. 4th Finger Intonation: Measures 5-6

©2026 C. Harvey Publications® All Rights Reserved.

The Bach Cello Suite No. 2 Study Book - Prelude

20. Shifting to Fourth Position: Measure 7

21. Shifting I: Measure 8

©2026 C. Harvey Publications® All Rights Reserved.

The Bach Cello Suite No. 2 Study Book - Prelude

22. Shifting II: Measure 8

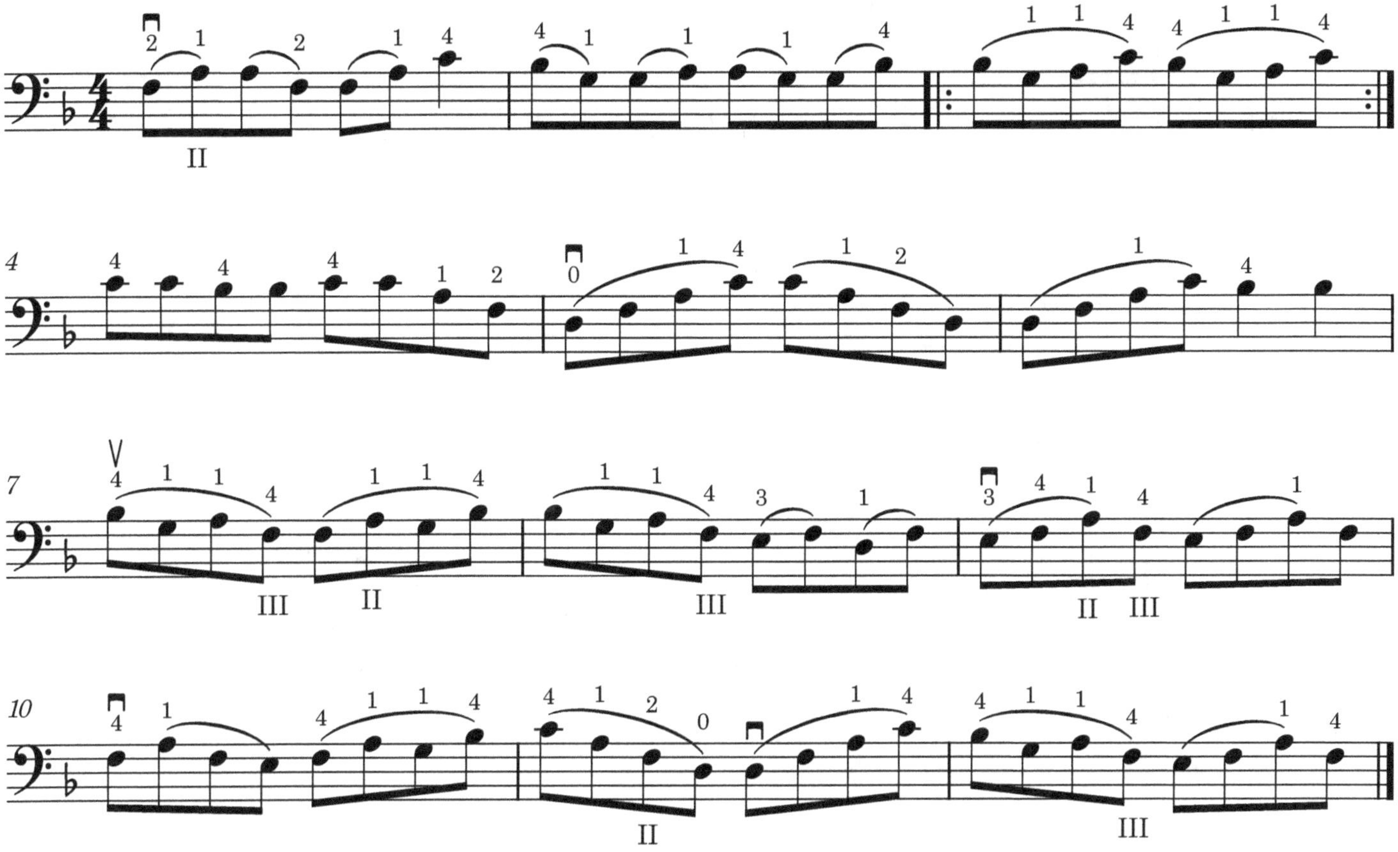

23. Intonation: Measures 7-8

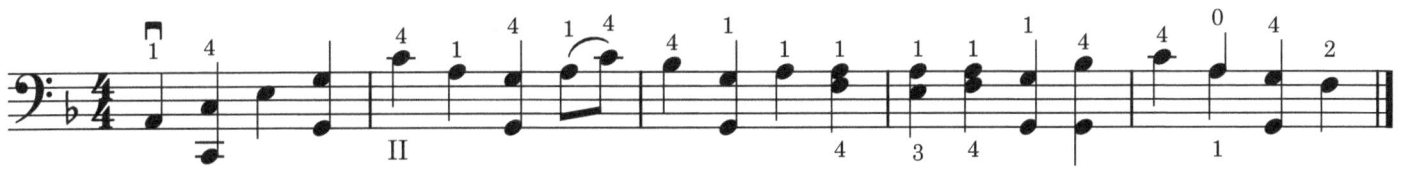

24. String Crossing I: Measures 5-8

No. 24-25: ♩ = 44–50

©2026 C. Harvey Publications® All Rights Reserved.

25. String Crossing II: Measures 5-8

Repeat each measure until comfortable.

26. *Prelude, Part Three*: Measures 9-12

27. Shifting Backwards to Second Position: Measures 8-9

Repeat until in tune.

The Bach Cello Suite No. 2 Study Book - Prelude

28. Shifting Back After an Open String: Measures 8-9

29. Shifting From Second to Third Position: Measure 9

©2026 C. Harvey Publications® All Rights Reserved.

30. Intonation: Measure 9

31. Shifting Backwards: Measure 9

The Bach Cello Suite No. 2 Study Book - Prelude

32. Bowing: Measures 8-10

33. Shifting I: Measure 10

34. Shifting II: Measure 10

©2026 C. Harvey Publications® All Rights Reserved.

35. Shifting and Bowing: Measure 10

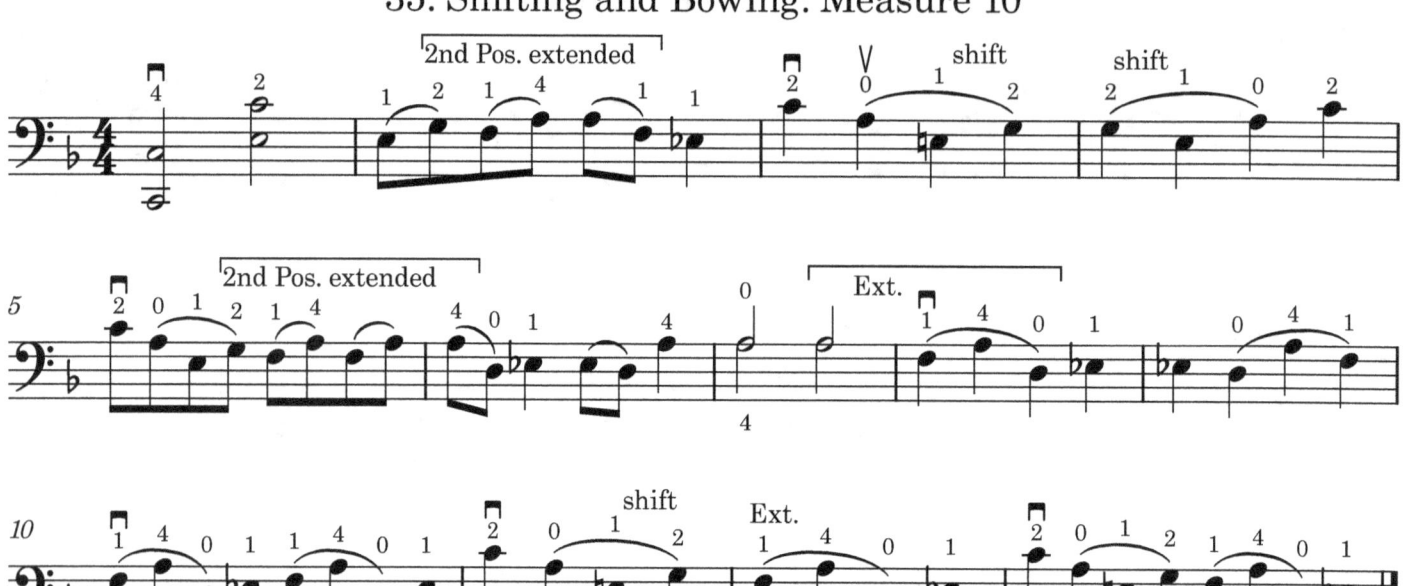

36. Intonation: Measure 10

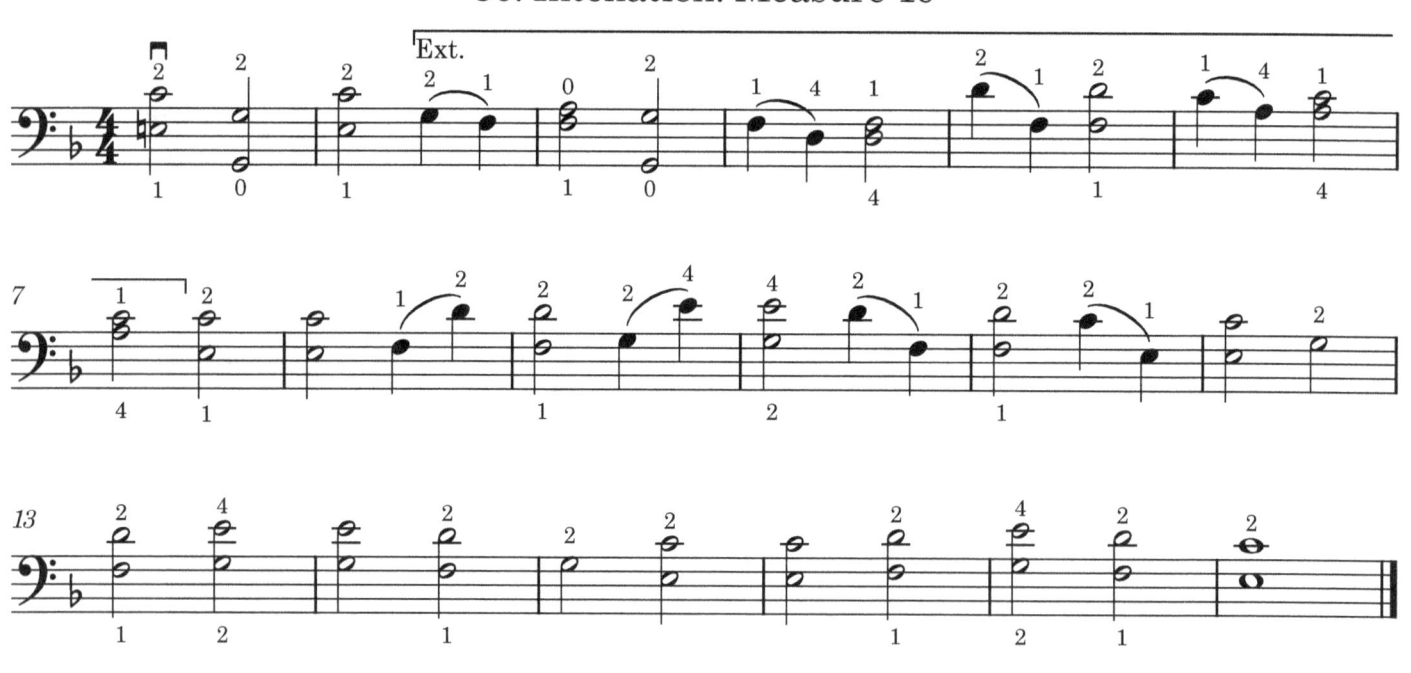

37. Bowing: Measures 9-10

The Bach Cello Suite No. 2 Study Book - Prelude

38. Intonation: Measure 11

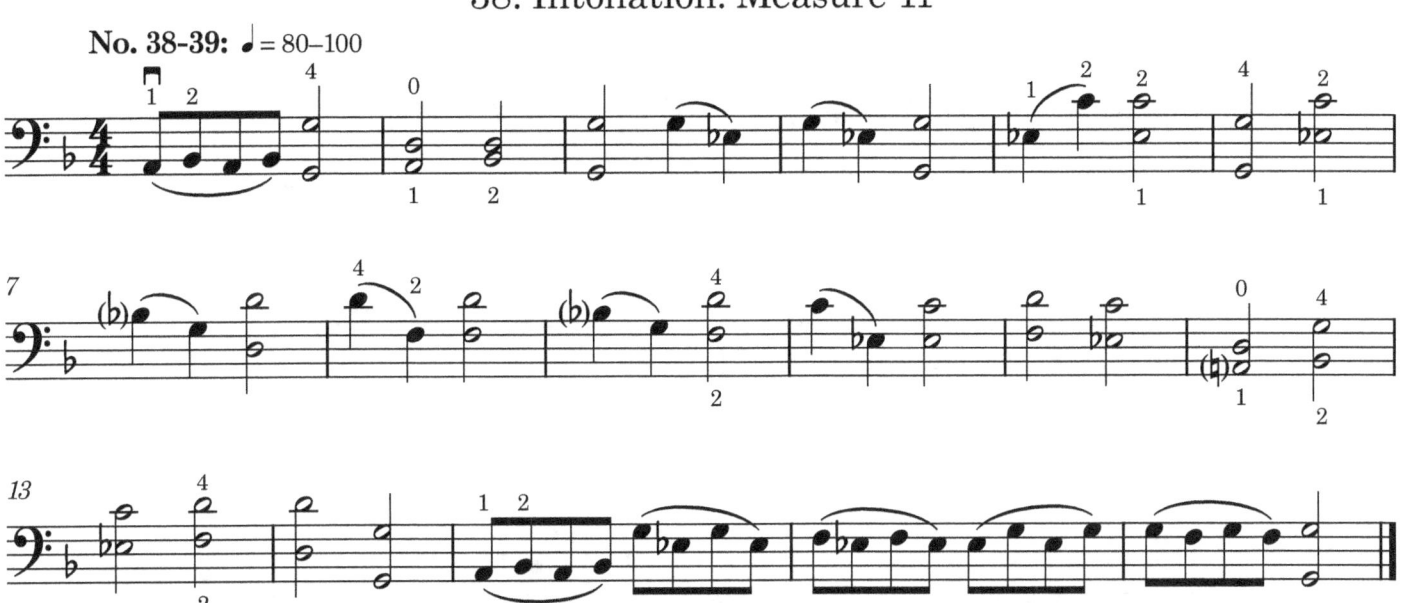

39. Hand Position Study: Measure 12

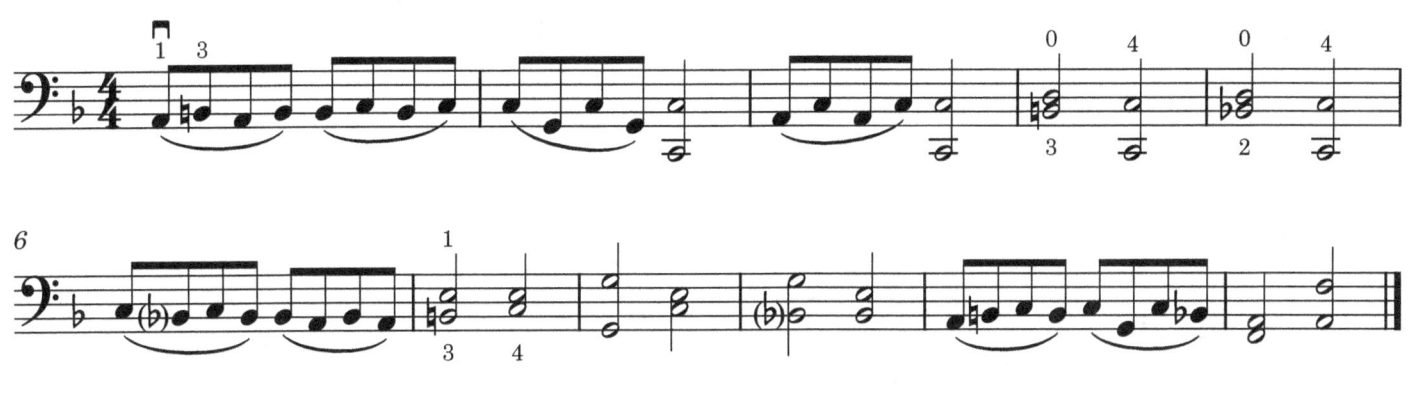

40. Bowing I: Measures 11-12

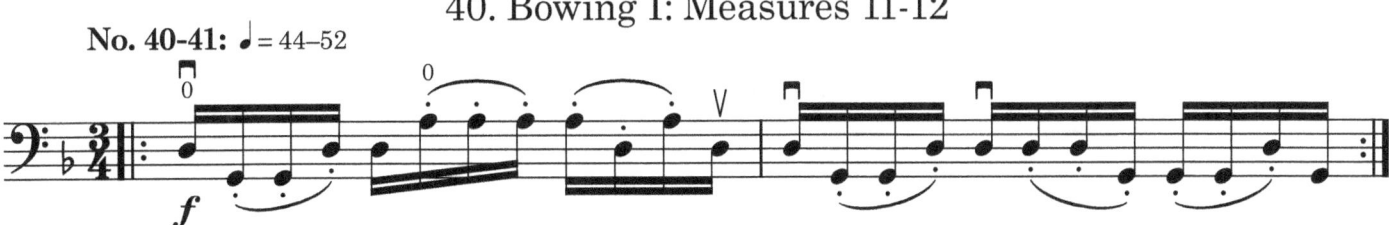

41. Bowing II: Measures 11-12

©2026 C. Harvey Publications® All Rights Reserved.

42. *Prelude, Part Four*: Measures 13-20

43. Intonation: Measures 13-14

The Bach Cello Suite No. 2 Study Book - Prelude

44. Bowing: Measures 12-14

45. Rhythm and Bowing : Measures 12-14

46. Shifting to Second Position: Measures 15-16

©2026 C. Harvey Publications® All Rights Reserved.

The Bach Cello Suite No. 2 Study Book - Prelude

47. Intonation: Measures 15-16

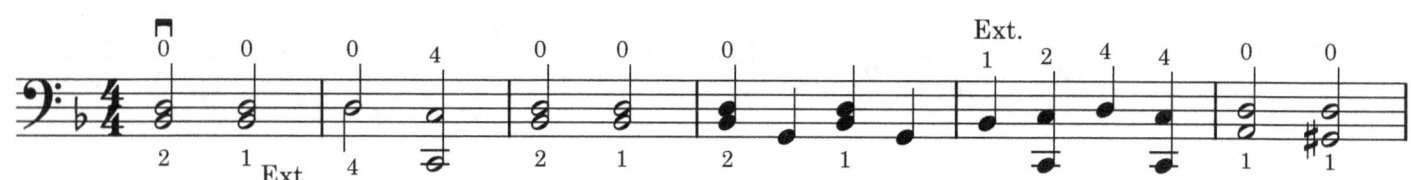

48. Bowing: Measures 15-16

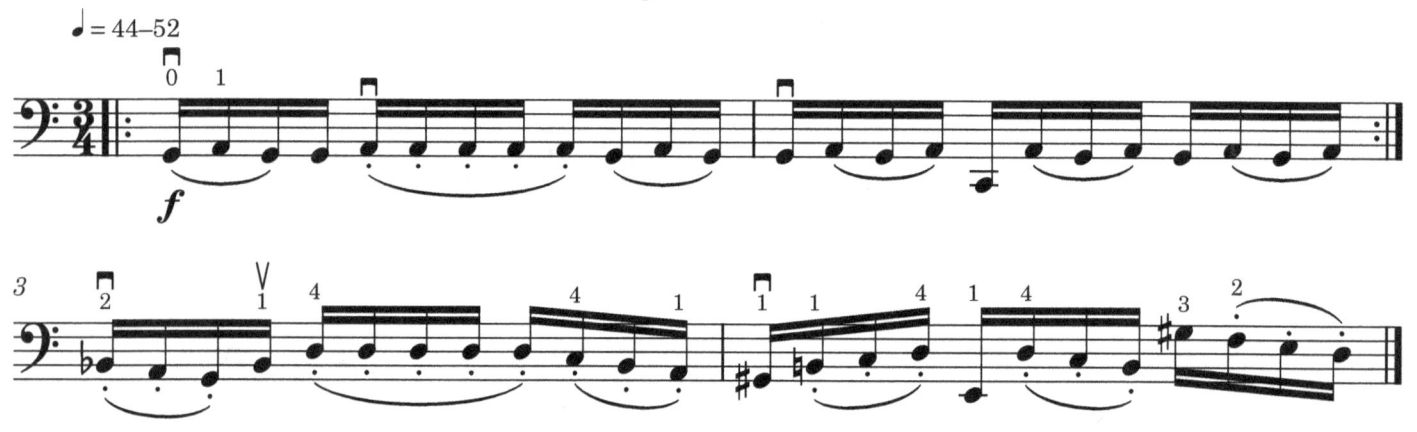

49. Shifting: Measure 17

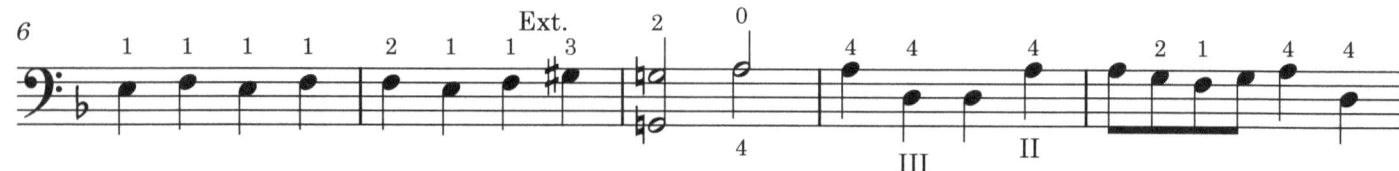

©2026 C. Harvey Publications® All Rights Reserved.

The Bach Cello Suite No. 2 Study Book - Prelude

50. Extending Across Strings: Measures 17-18

51. Shifting Back to Extended First Position: Measures 17-18

©2026 C. Harvey Publications® All Rights Reserved.

52. Fluency I: Measures 17-18

53. Fluency II: Measures 17-18

54. Shifting and String Crossing: Measure 19

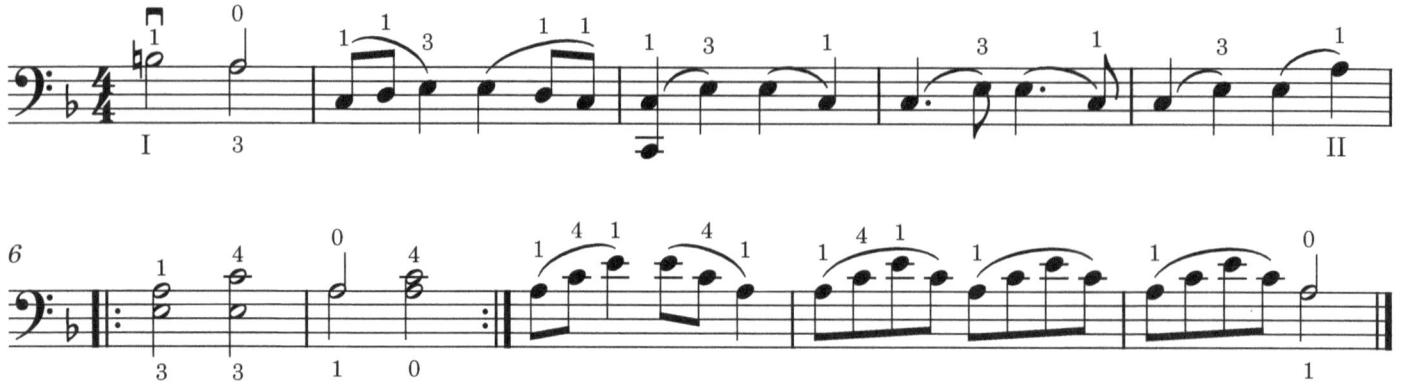

The Bach Cello Suite No. 2 Study Book - Prelude

55. Shifting Back on 4th Finger: Measure 19

56. Third Position Shifting: Measures 19-20

©2026 C. Harvey Publications® All Rights Reserved.

57. Rhythmic Shifting: Measures 19-20

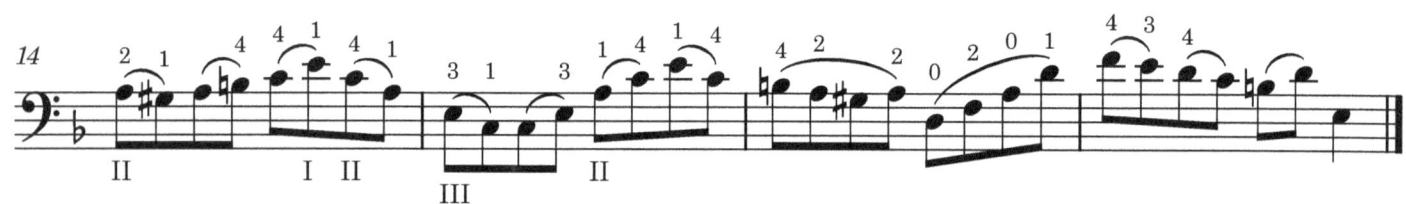

58. *Prelude, Part Five*: Measures 21-29

The Bach Cello Suite No. 2 Study Book - Prelude

59. Bowing: Measures 21-27

60. Intonation Across Strings: Measure 21

61. Shifting to Third Position: Measure 21

©2026 C. Harvey Publications® All Rights Reserved.

62. Shifting From Third to Second Position: Measures 21-22

63. Extended Second Position Across Strings: Measure 22

The Bach Cello Suite No. 2 Study Book - Prelude

64. In and Out of Half Position: Measure 23

65. Left Hand Agility and Intonation: Measures 24-25

©2026 C. Harvey Publications® All Rights Reserved.

66. Shifting to Second Position: Measure 25

67. Playing in Tune Across Strings: Measures 24-26

68. Shifting Into Extended Second Position: Measures 26-27

The Bach Cello Suite No. 2 Study Book - Prelude

69. Shifting From Second to Third Position: Measure 27

70. More Shifting Between Positions: Measures 25-27

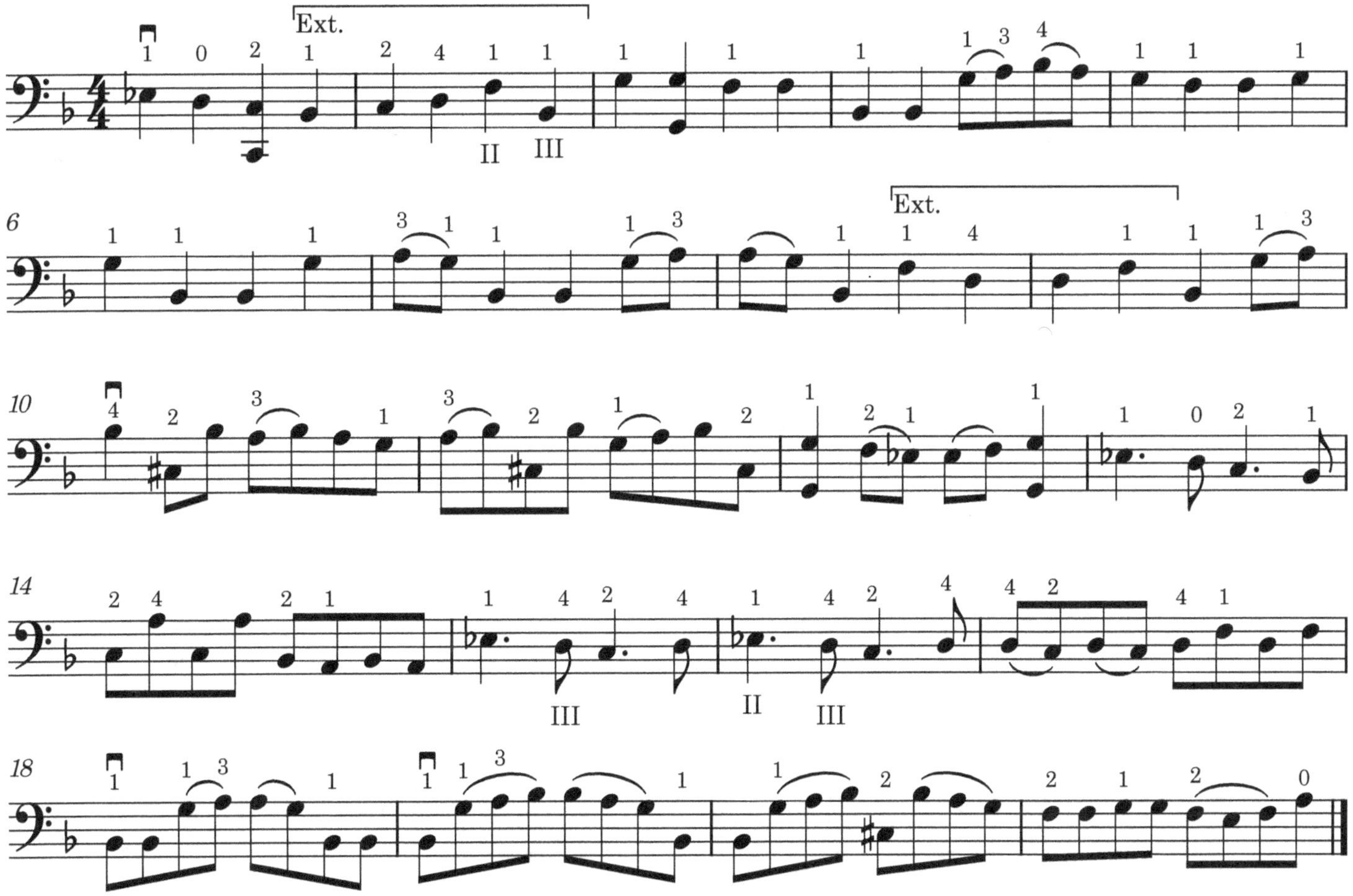

©2026 C. Harvey Publications® All Rights Reserved.

71. Learning to Shift Into Second Position: Measures 28-29

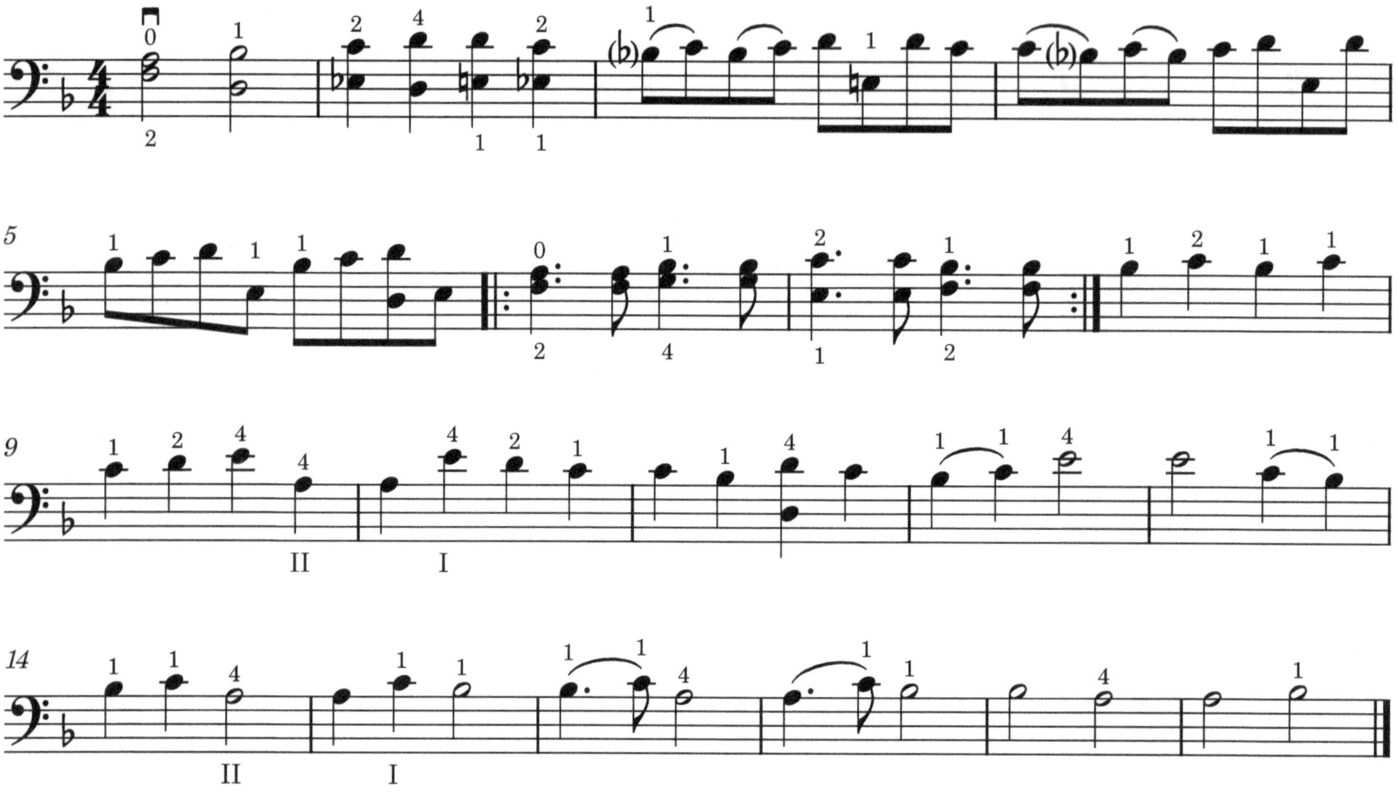

72. Shifting Into Second and Third Position: Measures 28-29

The Bach Cello Suite No. 2 Study Book - Prelude

73. Putting the Measures Together: Measures 27-29

74. *Prelude, Part Six*: Measures 30-35

©2026 C. Harvey Publications® All Rights Reserved.

The Bach Cello Suite No. 2 Study Book - Prelude

75. Finger Exercise: Measures 30-31

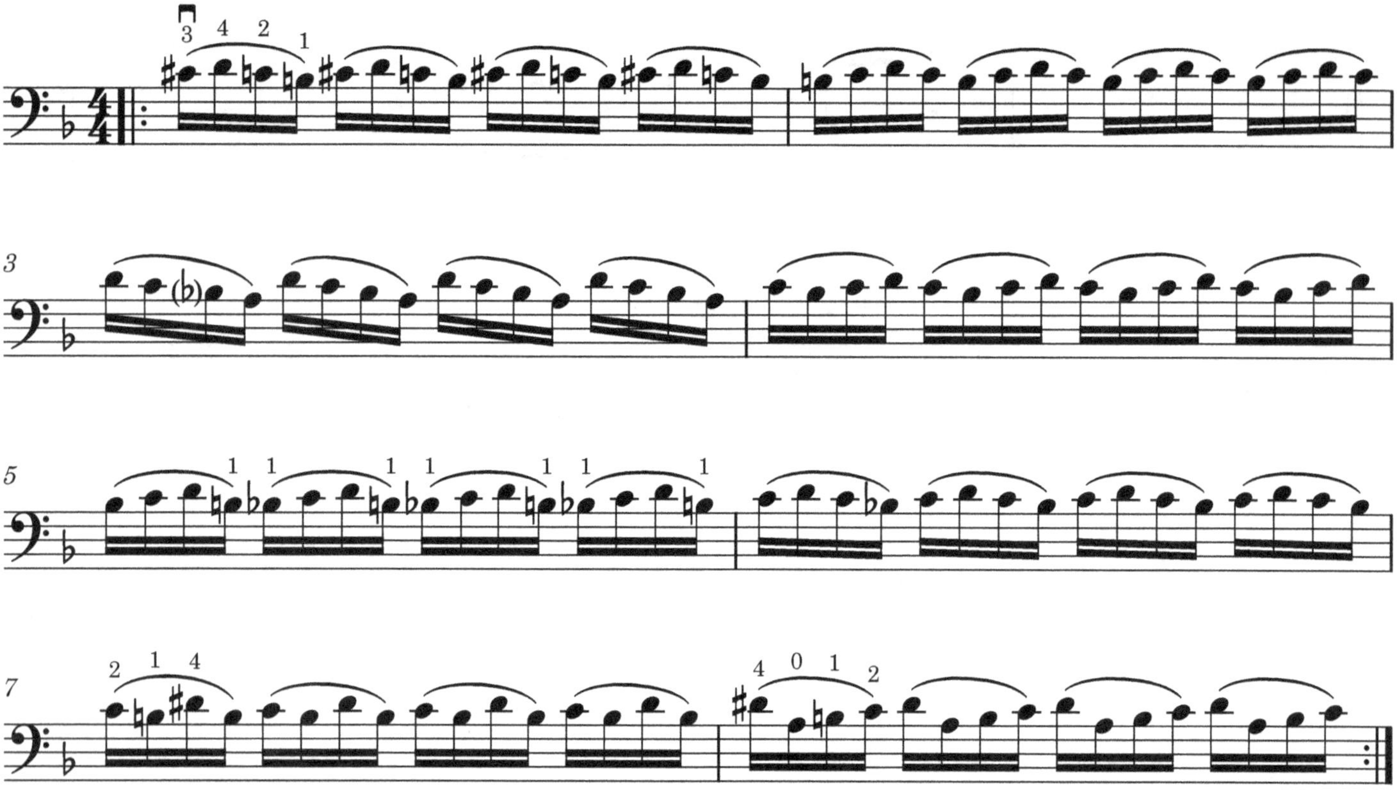

76. Shifting Into Extended Second Position: Measures 30-32

©2026 C. Harvey Publications® All Rights Reserved.

The Bach Cello Suite No. 2 Study Book - Prelude

77. Left and Right Hand Agility: Measures 30-31

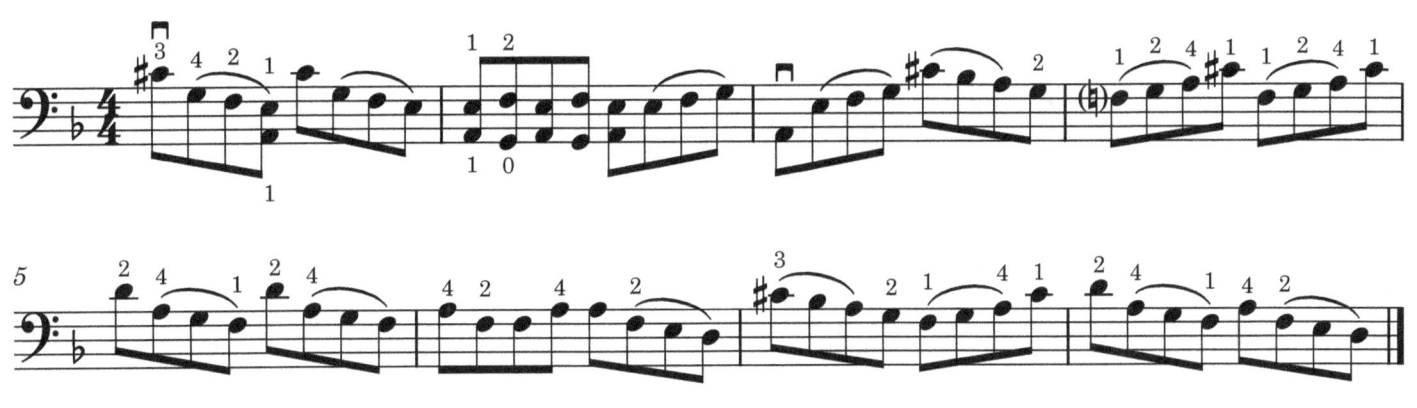

78. Awkward Extensions: Measure 32

Note: You may angle your left hand toward the bridge slightly to help you reach these extensions.

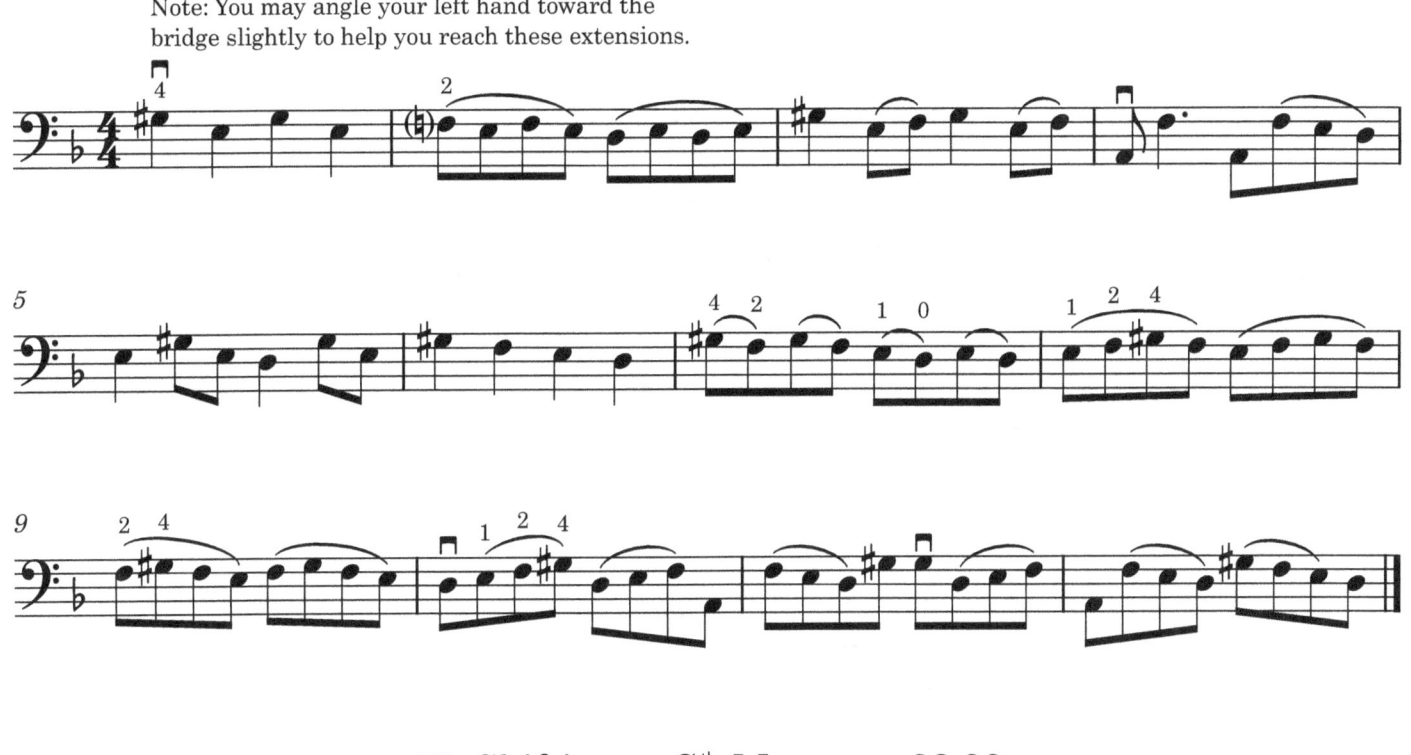

79. Shifting to C♯: Measures 32-33

©2026 C. Harvey Publications® All Rights Reserved.

80. Shifting From Second to Third Position: Measures 32-33

81. Fluency: Measures 32-33

82. Learning the Shift to Second Position: Measure 34

The Bach Cello Suite No. 2 Study Book - Prelude

83. Shifting Into Second Position: Measure 34

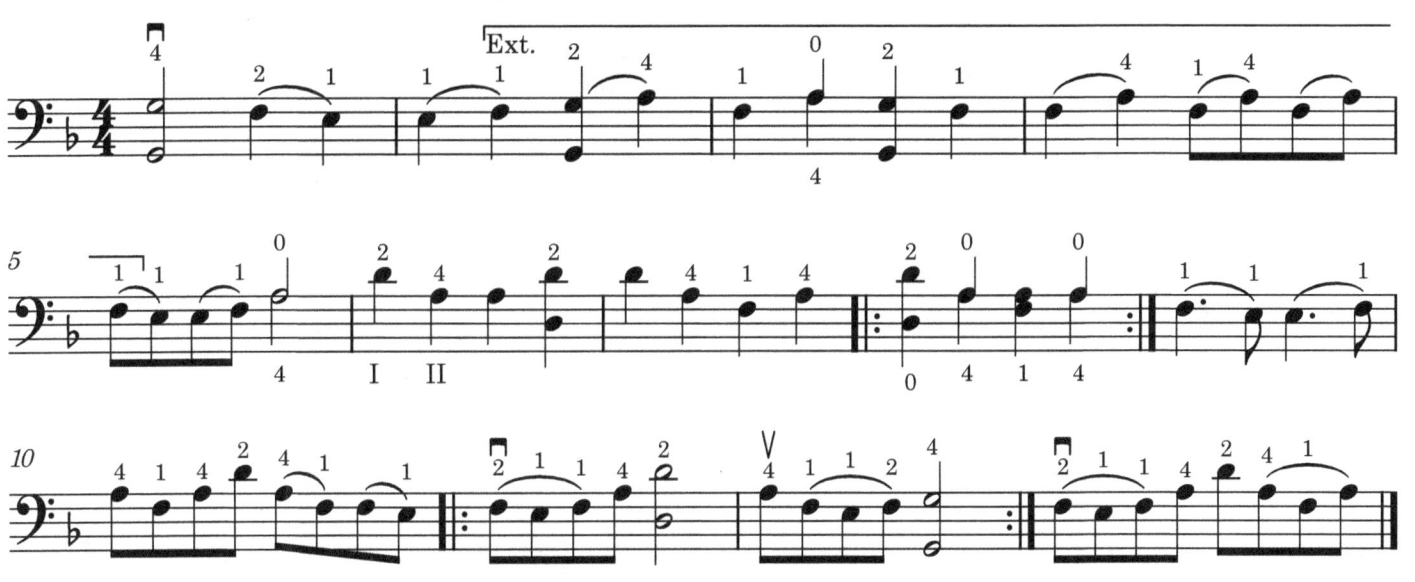

84. Shifting From Second to Fourth Position: Measures 34-35

85. Moving Across to Closed Second Position: Measure 35

©2026 C. Harvey Publications® All Rights Reserved.

86. Crossing Strings and Extending: Measure 35

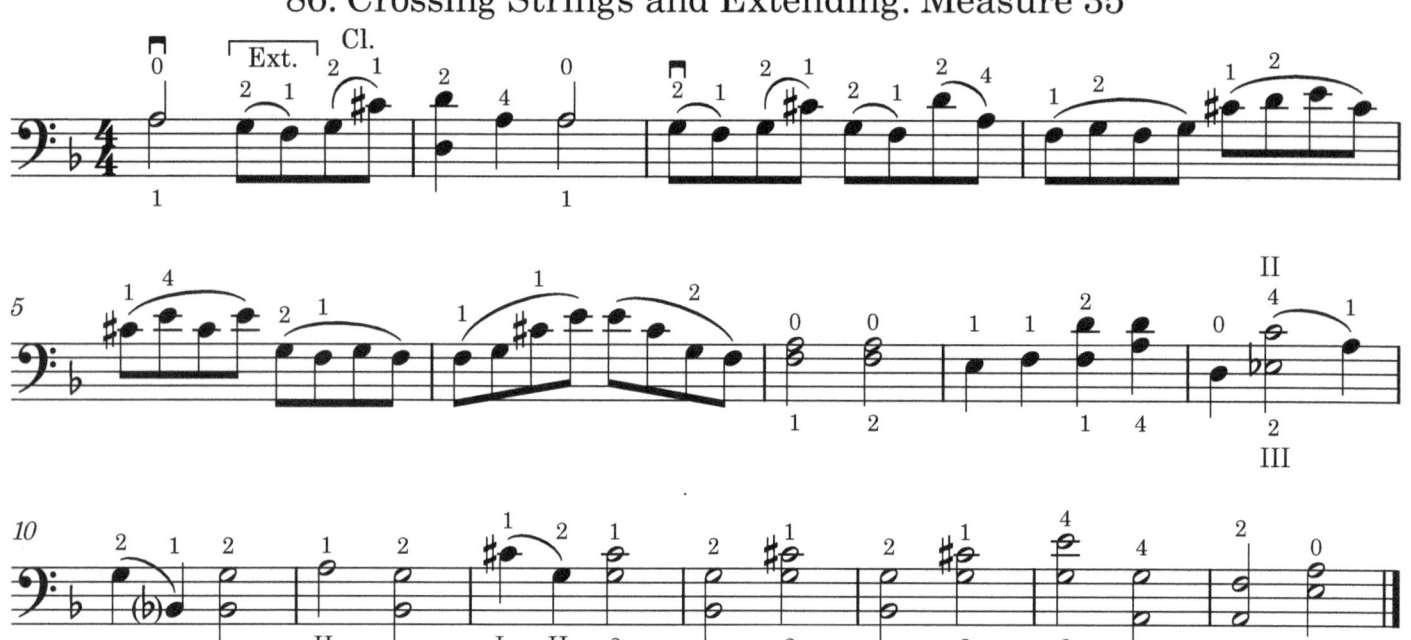

87. Bowing: Measures 30-35

88. *Prelude, Part Seven*: Measures 36-39

©2026 C. Harvey Publications® All Rights Reserved.

The Bach Cello Suite No. 2 Study Book - Prelude

89. Shifting to Third Position: Measure 36

No. 89-93: ♩ = 80–100

90. Shifting Between Third and Fourth Position: Measures 36-37

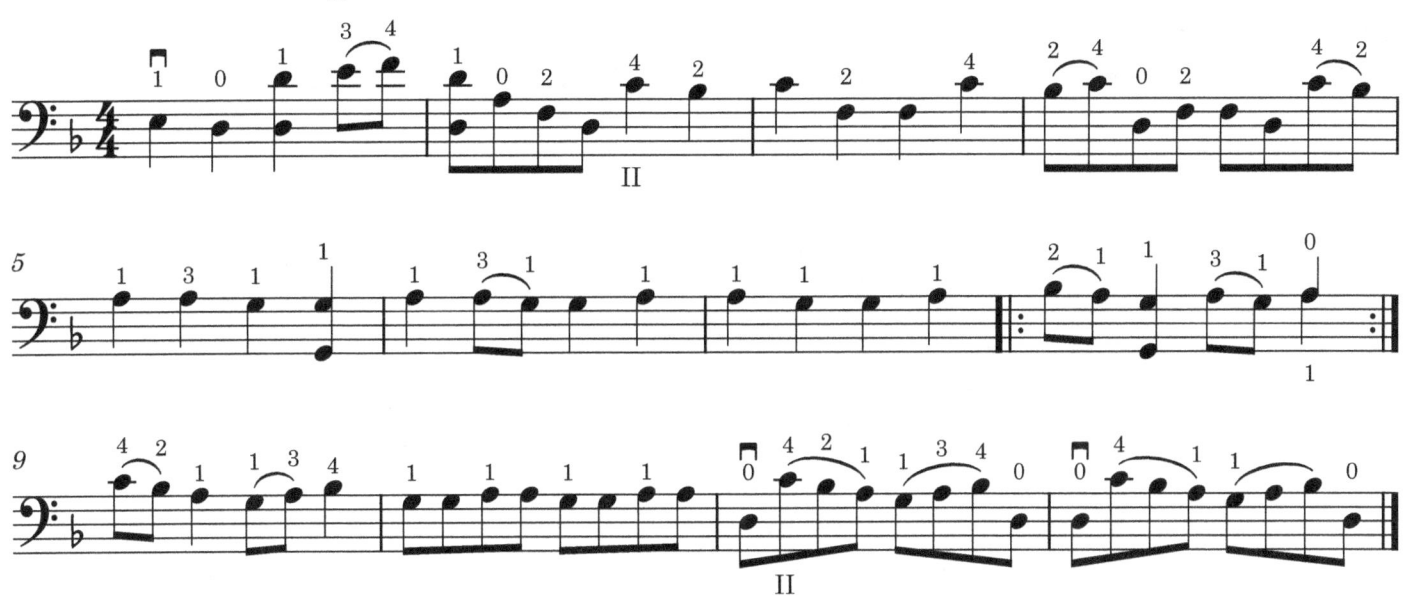

91. More Third Position: Measure 37

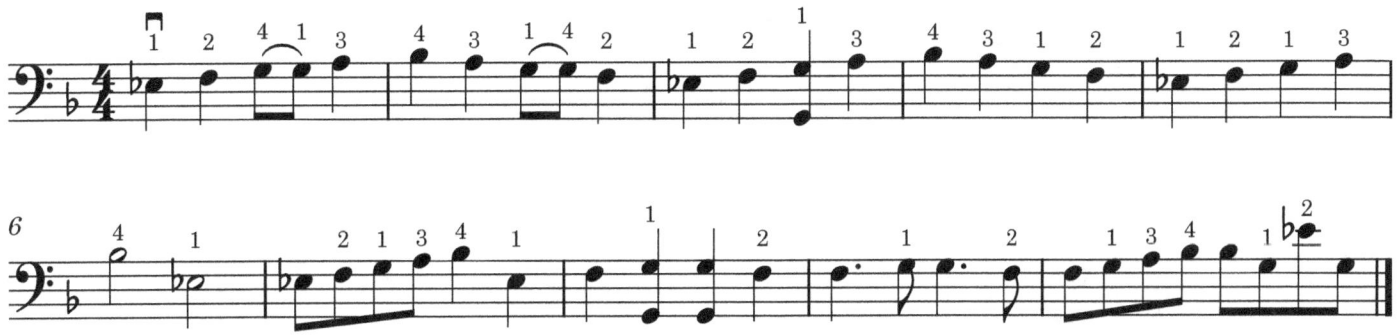

©2026 C. Harvey Publications® All Rights Reserved.

92. Shifting Back to Second Position: Measures 37-38

93. Agility: Measures 36-39

Thumb should move up and back under 2nd finger.

The Bach Cello Suite No. 2 Study Book - Prelude 37

94. *Prelude, Part Eight*: Measures 40-48

95. Moving In and Out of Half Position: Measure 40

©2026 C. Harvey Publications® All Rights Reserved.

96. Shifting to Extended Second Position: Measure 41

97. More Shifting to Extended Second Position: Measure 41

98. Agility: Measure 41

©2026 C. Harvey Publications® All Rights Reserved.

The Bach Cello Suite No. 2 Study Book - Prelude

99. Shifting Into Third Position: Measures 41-42

100. Landing Precisely After Open Strings: Measure 43

Make sure you play on the tips of your fingers for this exercise.
Carefully place your fingers on the string to train your hand
in the correct motions. A precisely stopped string will be less likely to squeak.

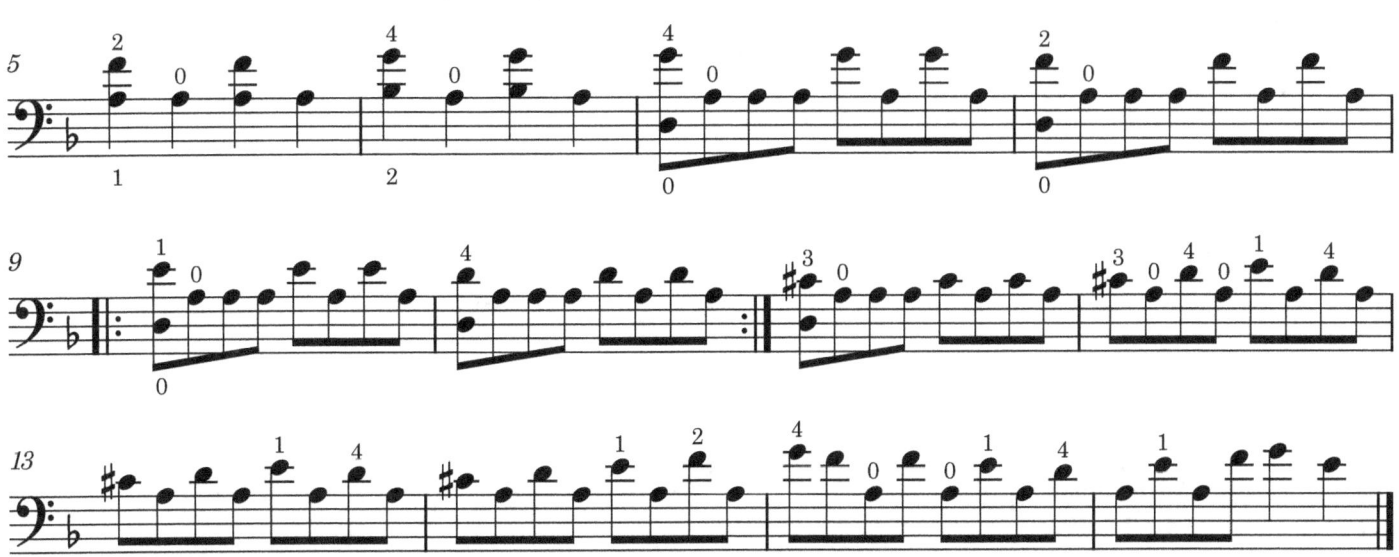

101. Shifting to Second Position: Measure 44

102. Fourth, Second, and Third Position: Measure 45

The Bach Cello Suite No. 2 Study Book - Prelude

105. *Prelude, Part Nine*: Measures 49-54

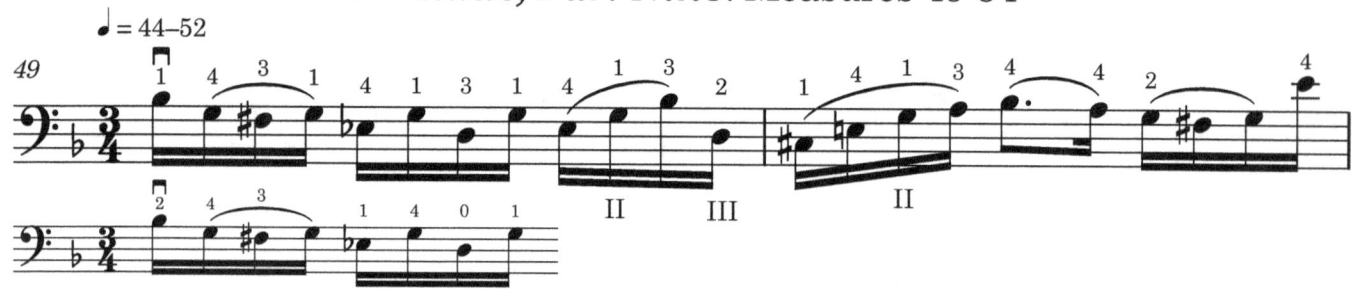

106. Extending Across Strings: Measure 49

©2026 C. Harvey Publications® All Rights Reserved.

The Bach Cello Suite No. 2 Study Book - Prelude

107. Extended and Closed Third Position: Measures 49-50

108. More Third Position Across Strings: Measures 49-50

109. Shifting Backwards on 4th Finger: Measure 50

110. Shifting Between Second and Third Position: Measures 50-51

111. Fluency: Measures 49-52

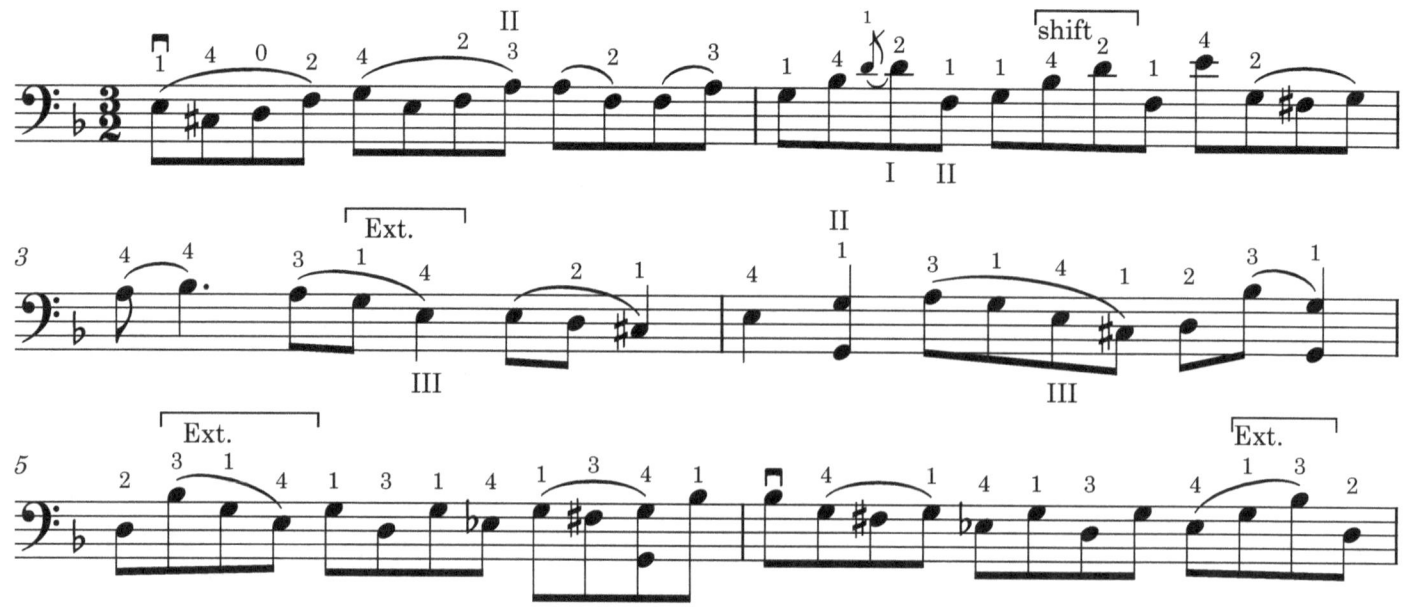

The Bach Cello Suite No. 2 Study Book - Prelude

112. Second Position: Measures 52-53

113. Playing the Chord: Measures 53-54

©2026 C. Harvey Publications® All Rights Reserved.

114. Bowing: Measures 49-54

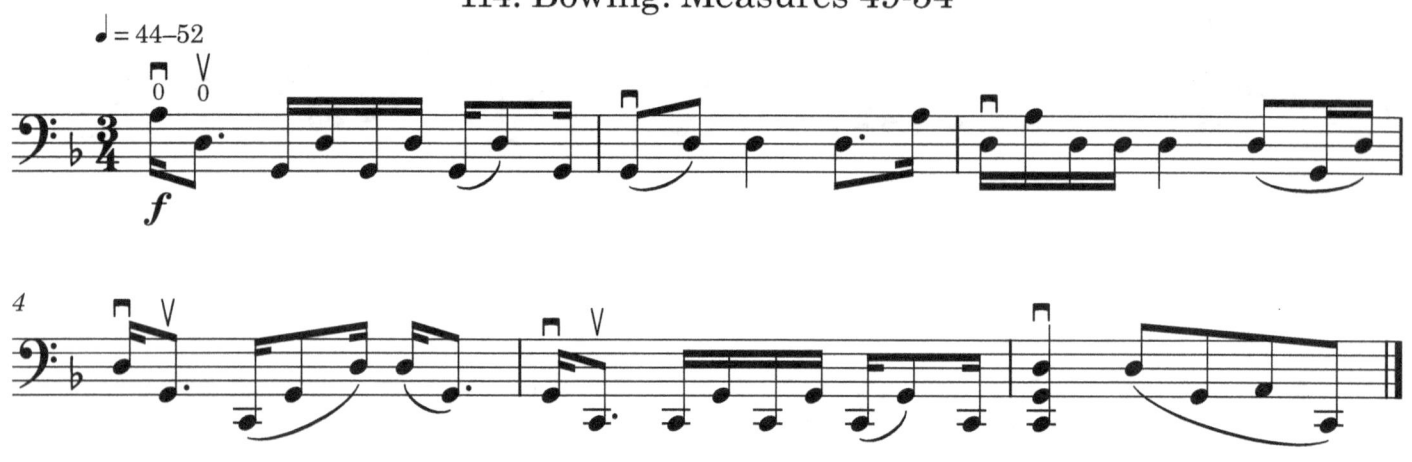

115. *Prelude, Part Ten*: Measures 55-63 (end)

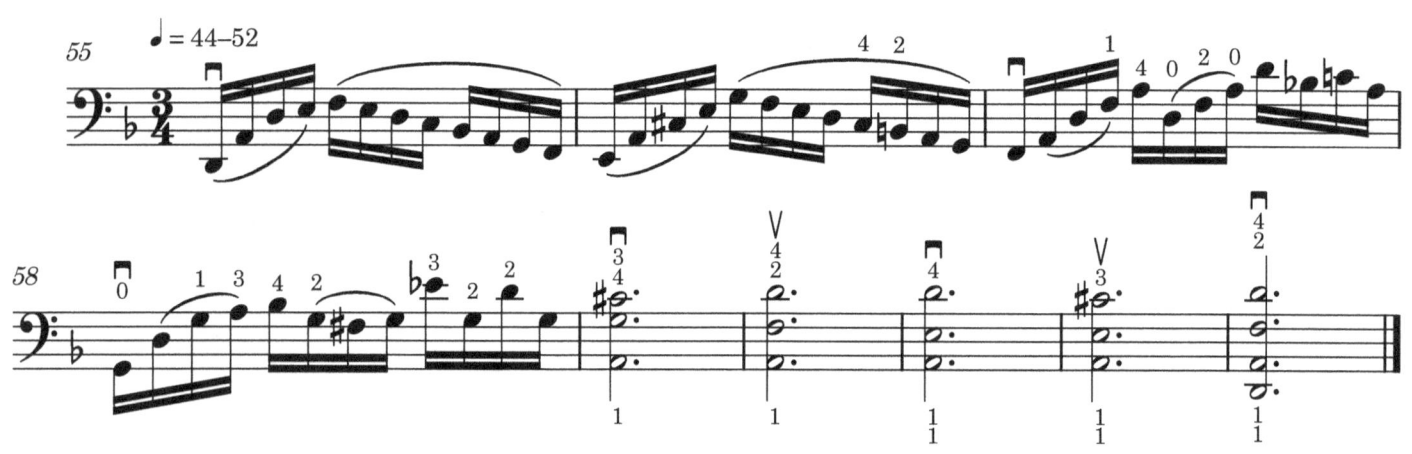

116. Bowing I: Measures 55-63

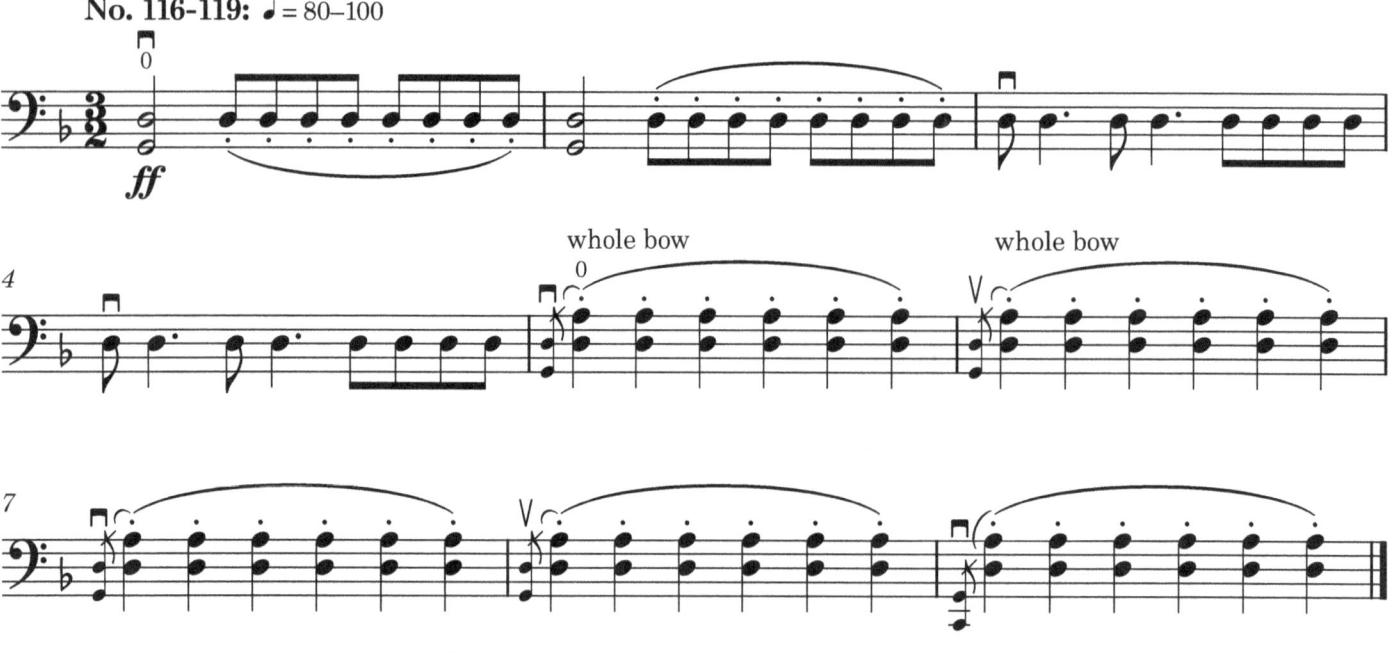

The Bach Cello Suite No. 2 Study Book - Prelude

117. Bowing II: Measures 55-63

118. Bowing III: Measures 55-56

119. Bowing IV: Measures 55-56

©2026 C. Harvey Publications® All Rights Reserved.

48 The Bach Cello Suite No. 2 Study Book - Prelude

120. Finger Exercise: Measures 55-56

121. Shifting to Second Position: Measure 56

©2026 C. Harvey Publications® All Rights Reserved.

The Bach Cello Suite No. 2 Study Book - Prelude

122. Shifting to Third Position: Measures 57-58

123. Intonation for Double Stops: Measures 59-63

124. Strength Training I for Double Stops: Measures 59-63

125. Strength Training II for Double Stops: Measures 59-63

©2026 C. Harvey Publications® All Rights Reserved.

The Bach Cello Suite No. 2 Study Book - Prelude

126. Prelude, Part Ten With Different Bowing on Chords: Measures 55-end

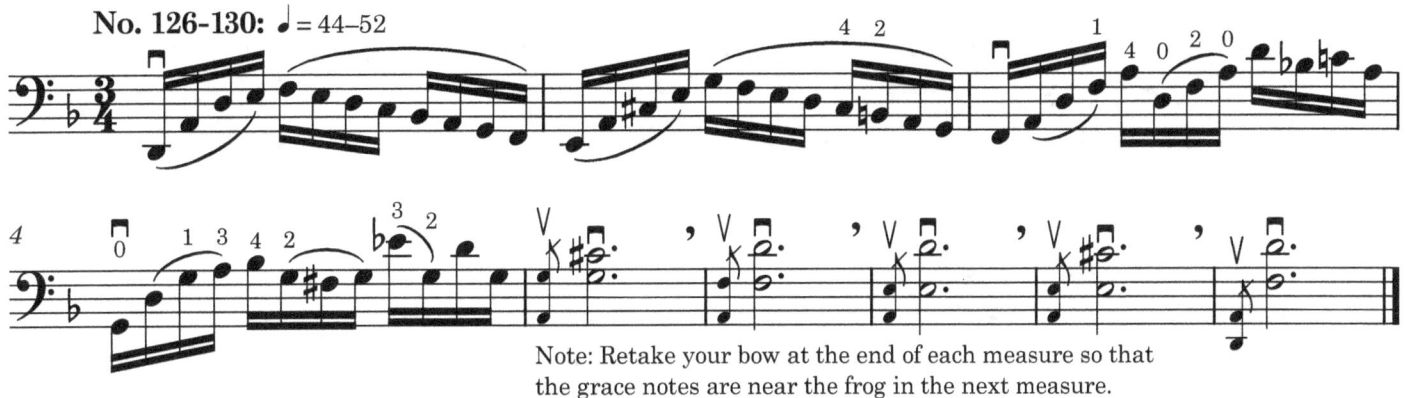

Note: Retake your bow at the end of each measure so that the grace notes are near the frog in the next measure.

127. Prelude, Part Ten With Arpeggiation Option 1: Friedrich Grutzmacher

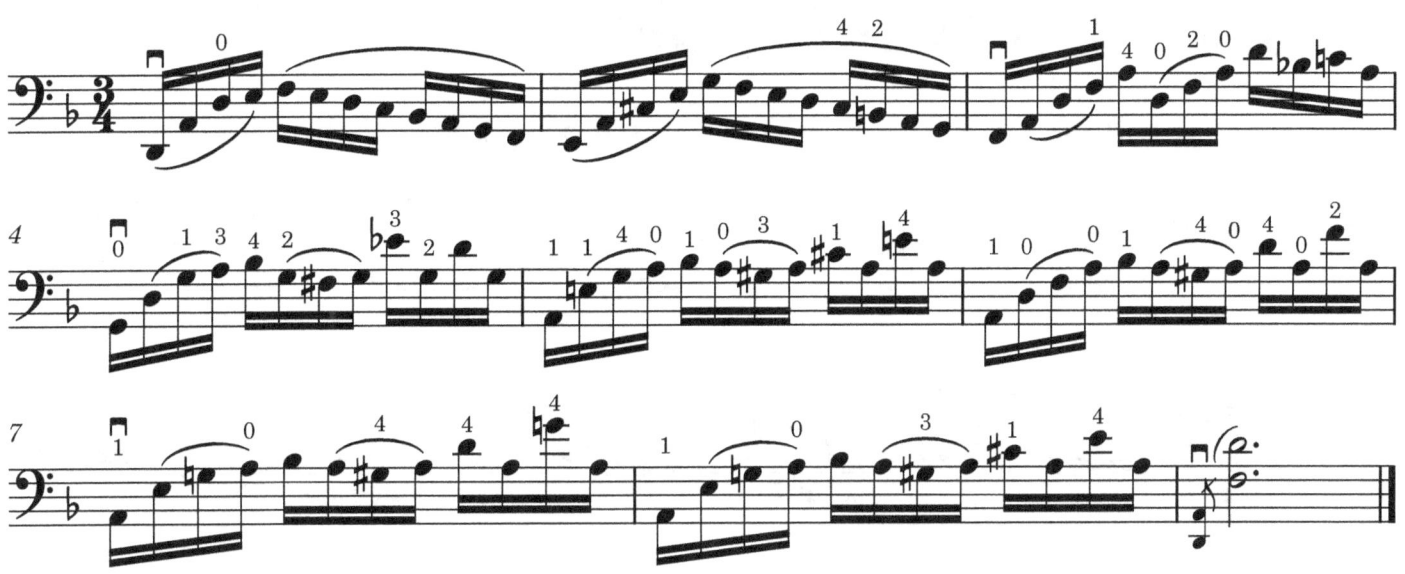

128. Prelude, Part Ten With Arpeggiation Option 2: Diran Alexanian

©2026 C. Harvey Publications® All Rights Reserved.

The Bach Cello Suite No. 2 Study Book - Allemande

132. Bowing: Measures 1-4

Keep bow on the string for this exercise.

133. Flattened and Curved Fingers: Measure 1

134. Learning the Chord: Measure 1

Note: Pivot silently across strings when the bow changes direction here; the bow should not leave the string.

©2026 C. Harvey Publications® All Rights Reserved.

135. Shifting to Third Position: Measure 1

136. Shifting to Third and Second Position: Measure 2

137. Fluency: Measures 1-2

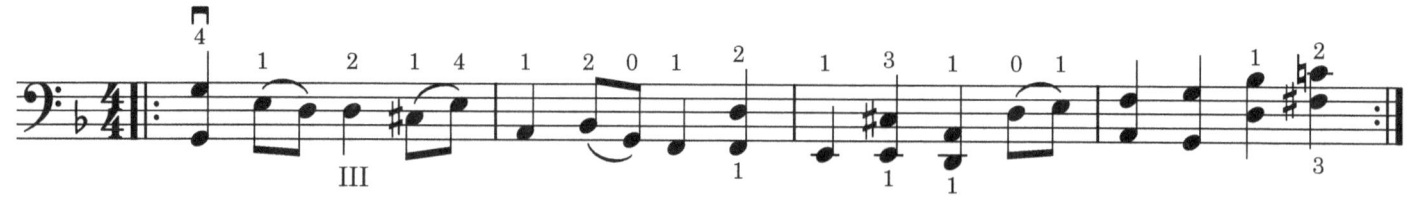

The Bach Cello Suite No. 2 Study Book - Allemande

138. Transitions to Chords: Measures 1-3

139. Shifting to Second Position From a Chord: Measure 3

140. Shifting to Third Position: Measure 4

©2026 C. Harvey Publications® All Rights Reserved.

141. Bowing: Measures 1-4

142. *Allemande, Part Two*: Measures 5-8

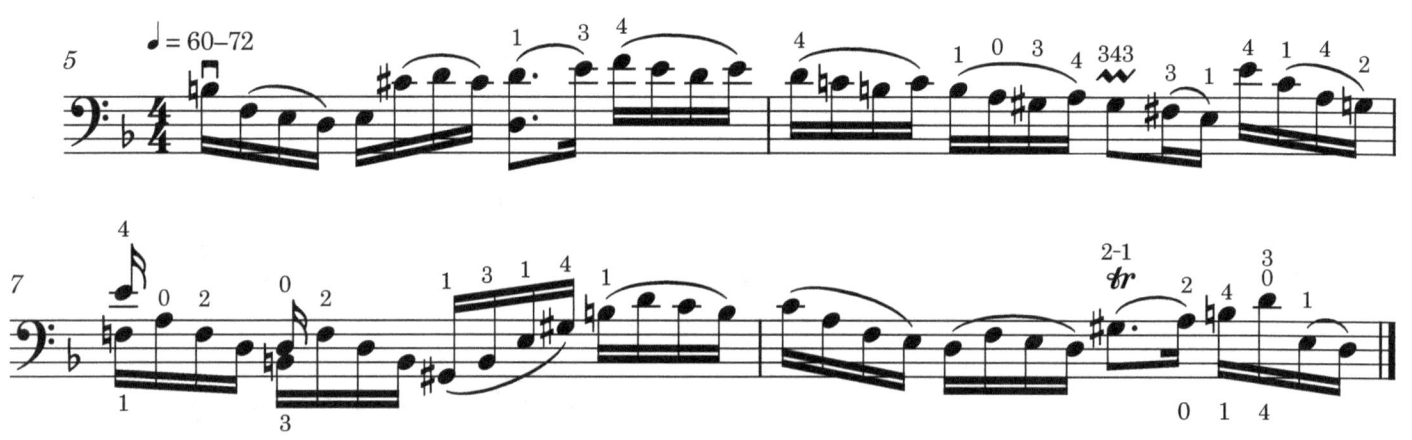

143. Shifting to Third Position: Measure 5

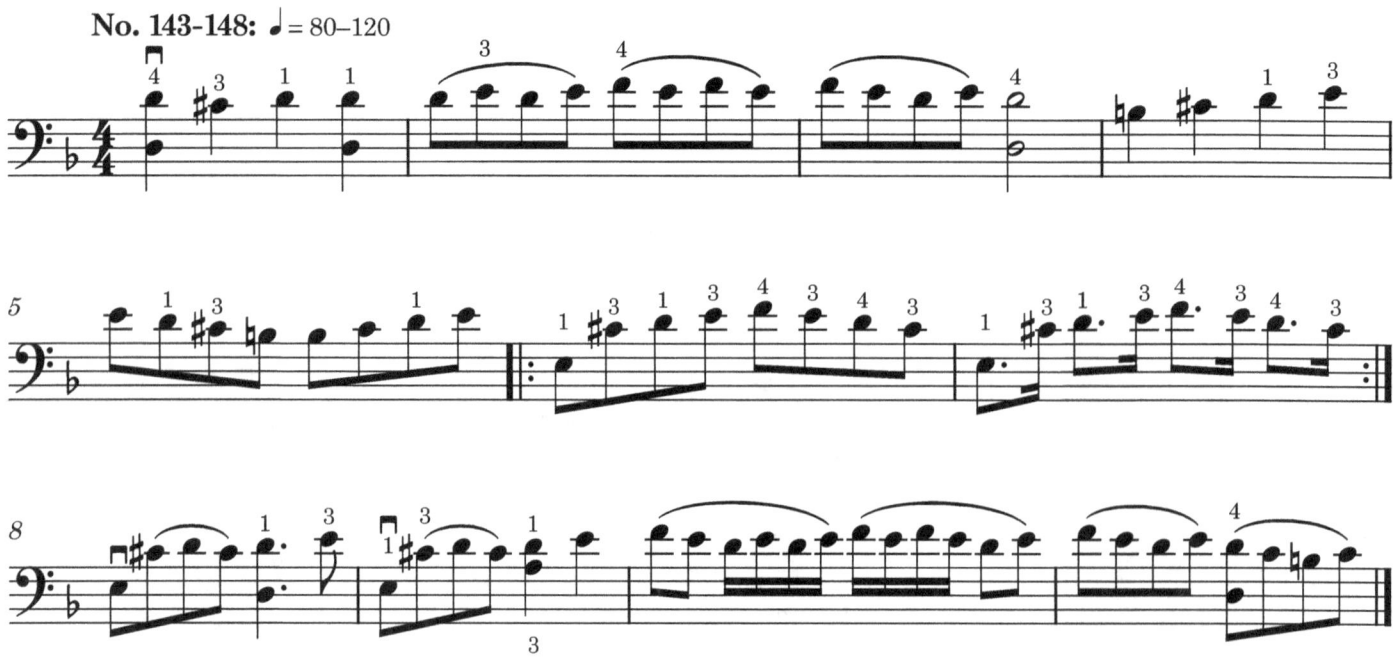

The Bach Cello Suite No. 2 Study Book - Allemande 57

144. Learning the Shifts: Measures 5-6

145. Shifting to Extended Second Position: Measures 6-7

©2026 C. Harvey Publications® All Rights Reserved.

The Bach Cello Suite No. 2 Study Book - Allemande

146. More Extended Second Position: Measures 6-7

147. Moving Across Strings With the Left Hand: Measures 7-8

The Bach Cello Suite No. 2 Study Book - Allemande

148. Shifting to the Trill: Measure 8

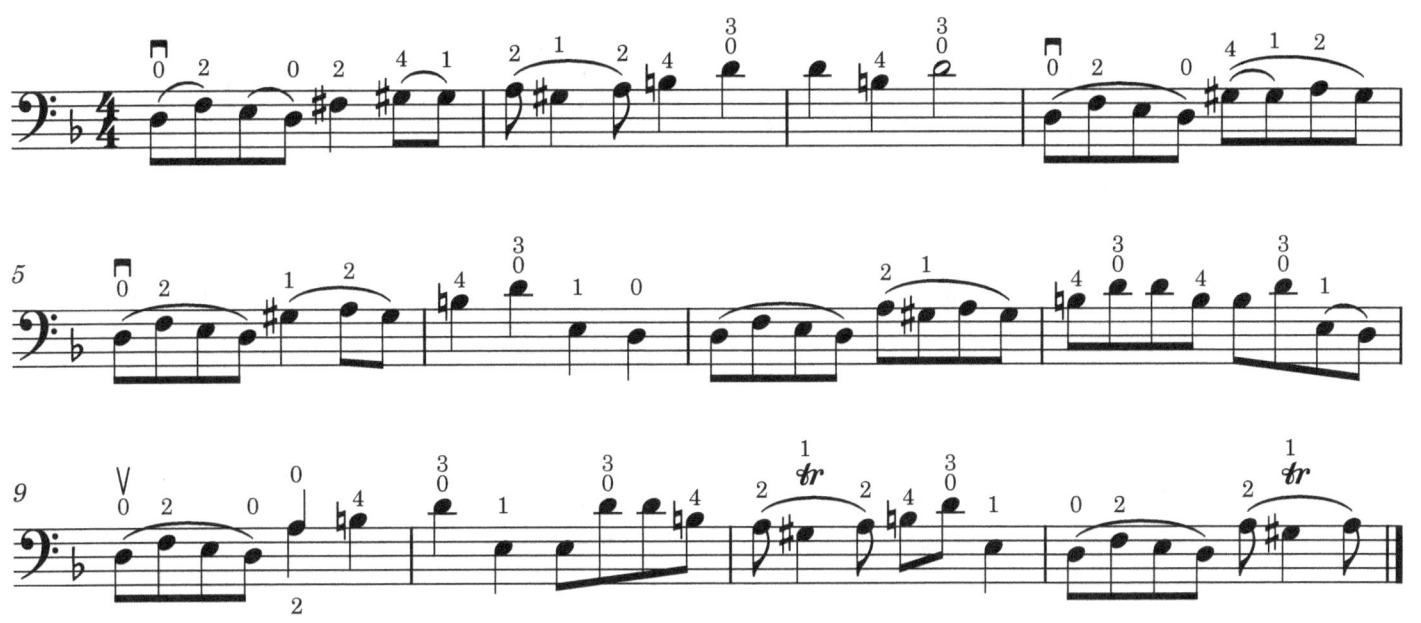

149. *Allemande, Part Three*: Measures 9-12

150. Trill Study No. 1: Measure 9

151. Trill Study No. 2: Measure 9

152. Finger Exercise for Speed: Measure 9

No. 152-156: ♩ = 80–120

Repeat several times, getting faster each time.

The Bach Cello Suite No. 2 Study Book - Allemande

153. Speed: Measure 9

Repeat several times, getting faster each time.

154. Fluency: Measure 9

Repeat several times, getting faster each time.

155. Rhythm and Bowing: Measure 9

©2026 C. Harvey Publications® All Rights Reserved.

156. Quick Shifting to Third Position: Measure 10

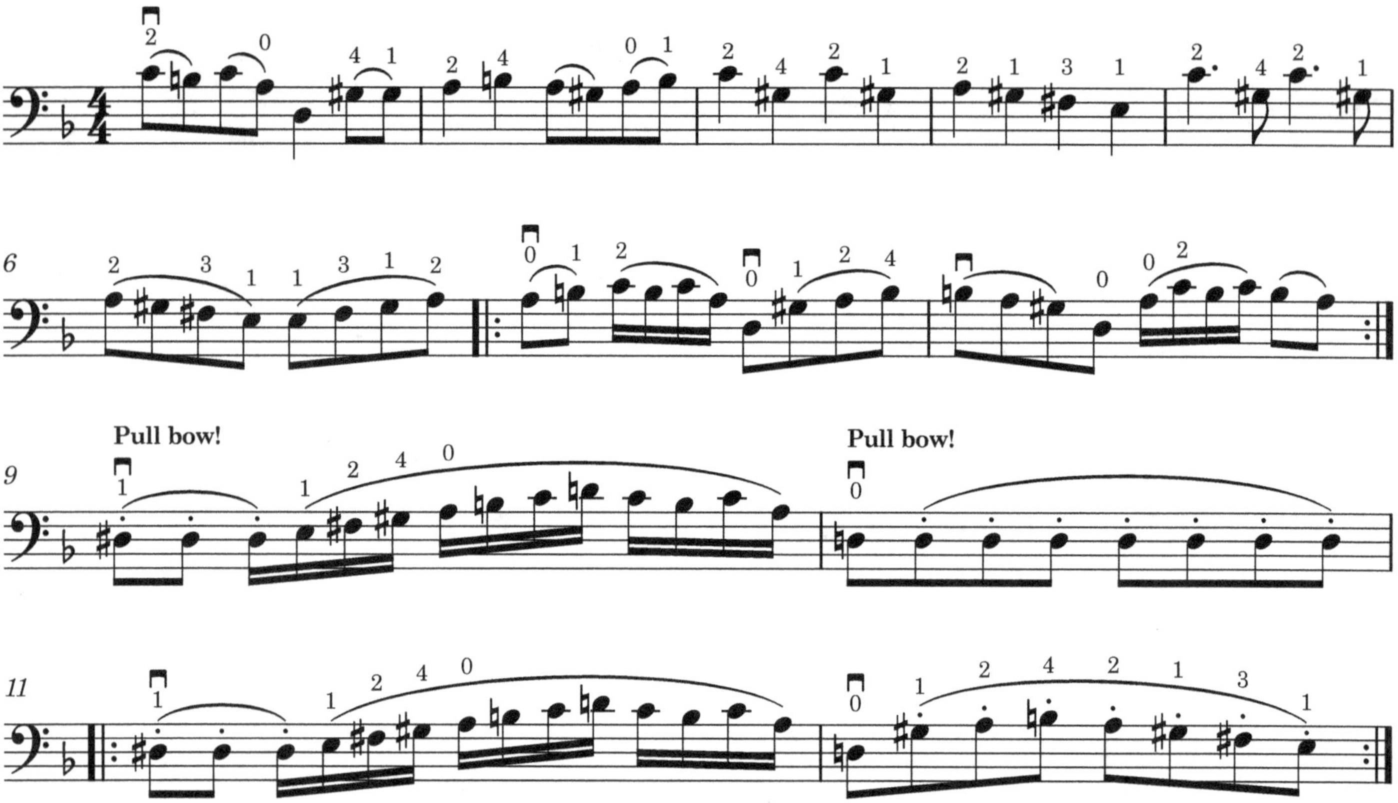

157. Chords and Second Position: Measures 10-12

The Bach Cello Suite No. 2 Study Book - Allemande

158. *Allemande, Part Four*: Measures 13-16

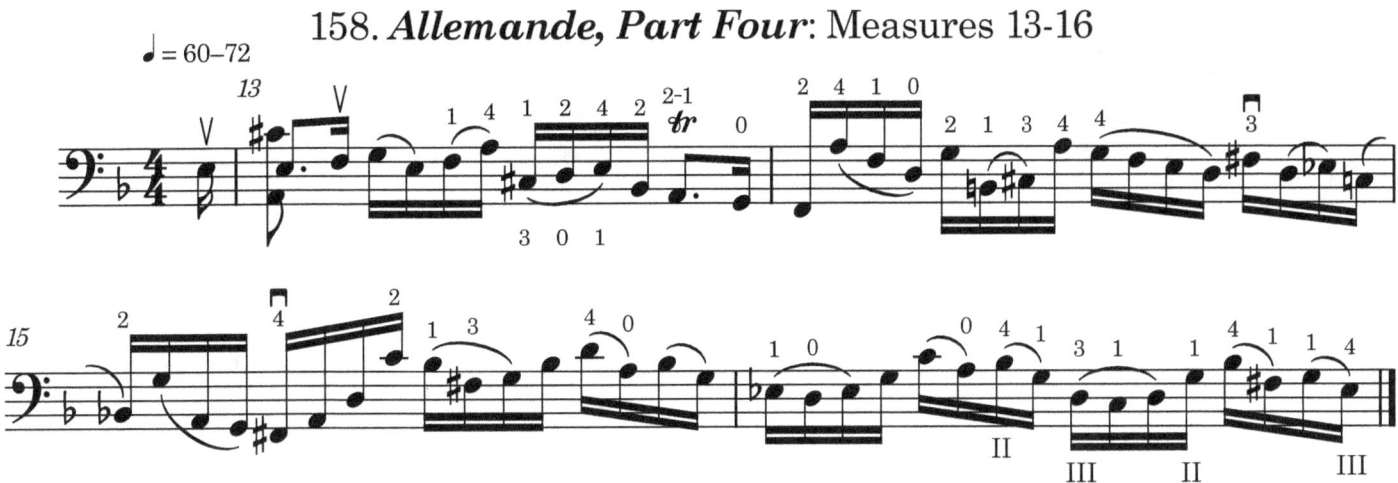

159. Bowing: Measures 13-16

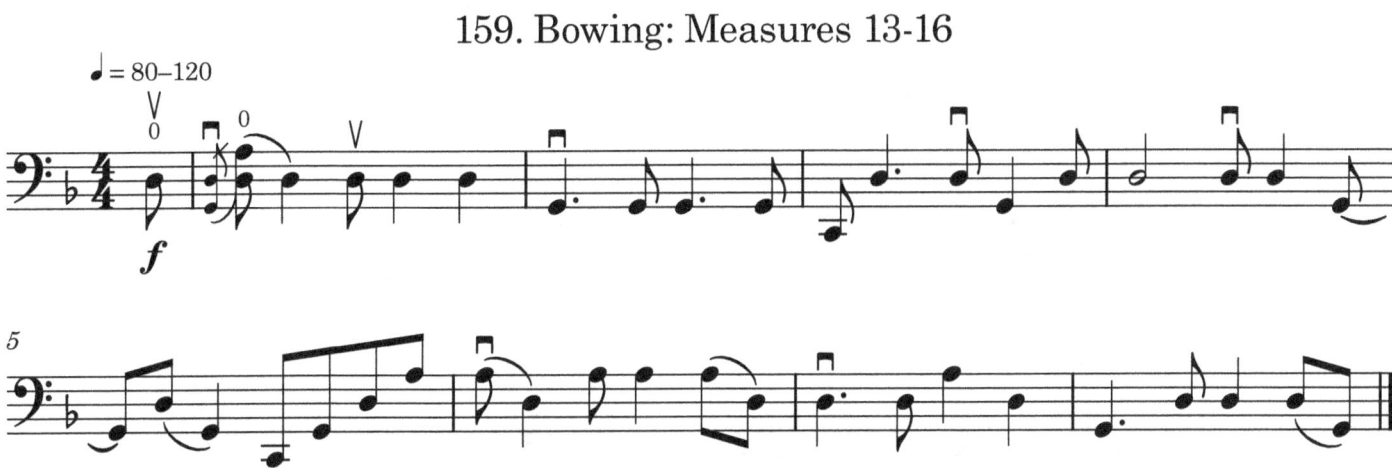

160. Chord: Measure 13

©2026 C. Harvey Publications® All Rights Reserved.

The Bach Cello Suite No. 2 Study Book - Allemande

161. Shifting to Second and Third Position: Measure 13

162. Intonation: Measure 13

163. Shifting From an Open String: Measure 14

164. Extensions Across Strings: Measure 14

©2026 C. Harvey Publications® All Rights Reserved.

The Bach Cello Suite No. 2 Study Book - Allemande

165. Intonation and Bowing: Measures 14-15

166. Shifting to Third Position Across Strings: Measure 16

©2026 C. Harvey Publications® All Rights Reserved.

167. *Allemande, Part Five*: Measures 17-20

168. Learning the Shifts: Measure 17

No. 168-173: ♩ = 80–110

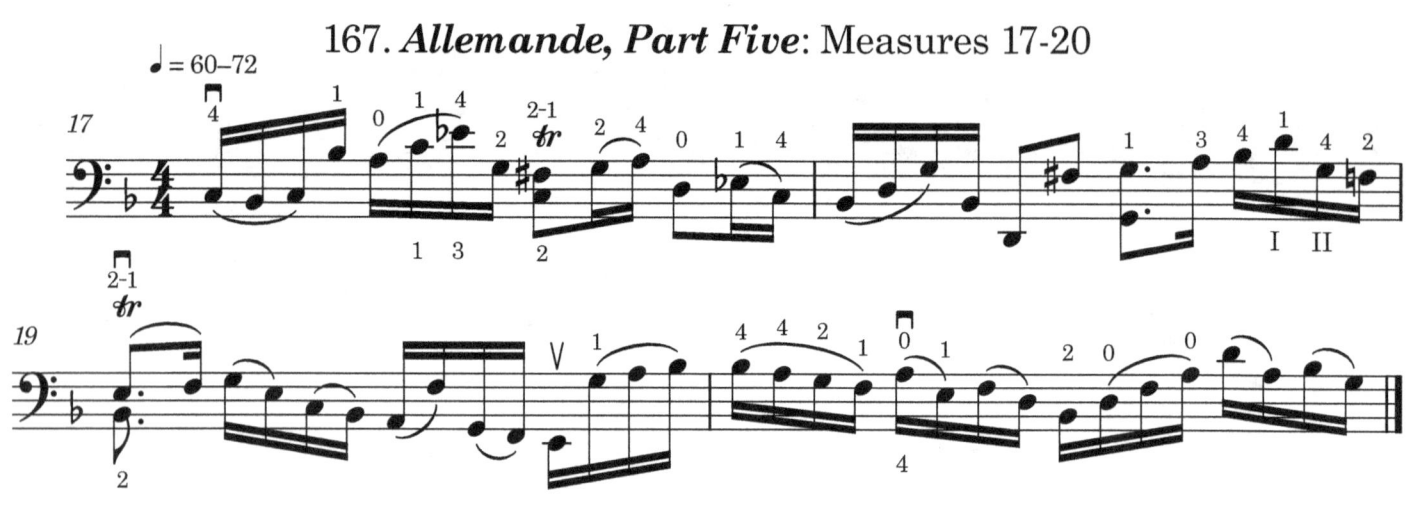

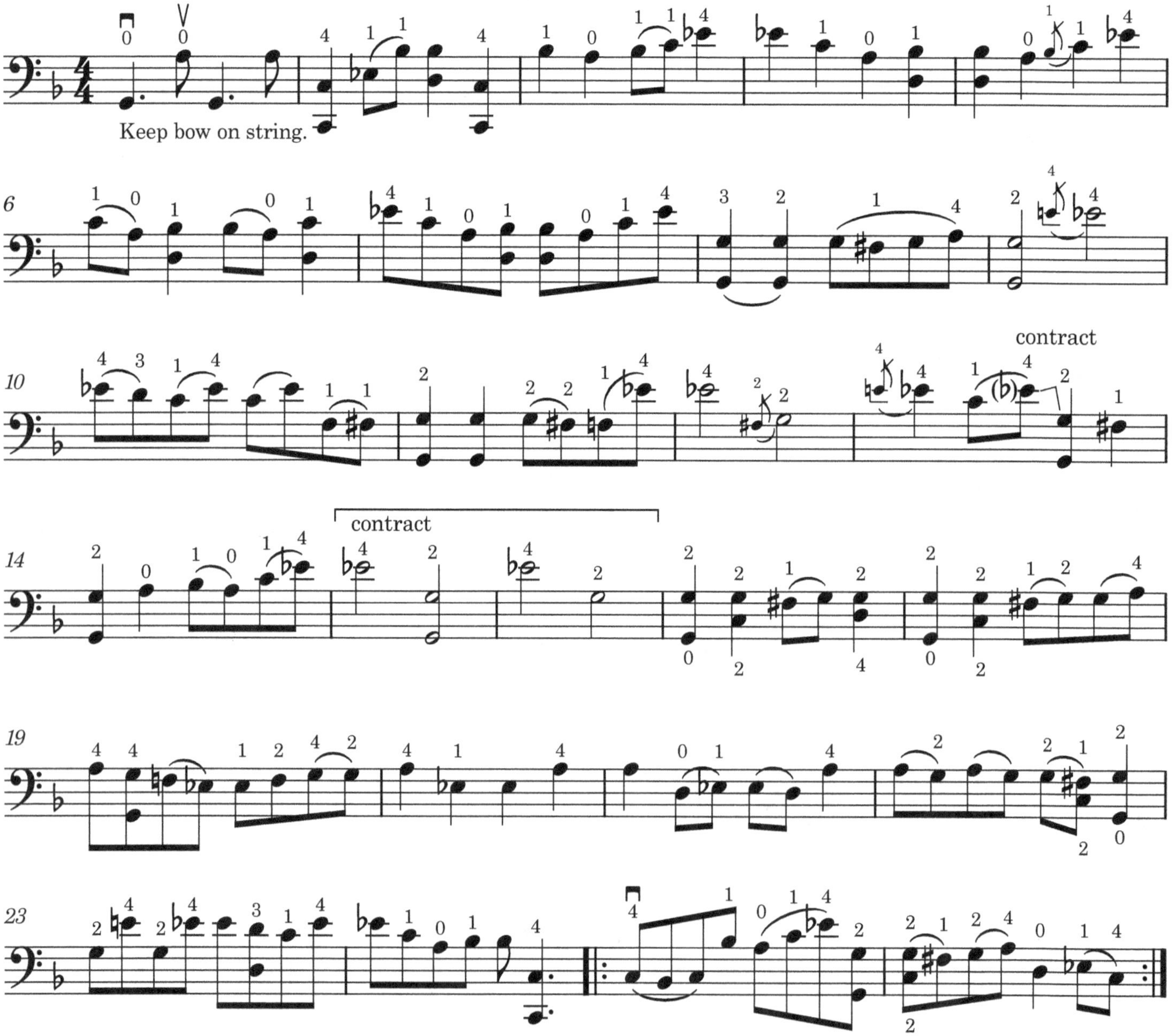

The Bach Cello Suite No. 2 Study Book - Allemande   67

169. Working on Two Trills: Measures 17, 19

170. Keeping Fingers Curved: Measure 18

171. Awkward Bowing I: Measures 19-20

172. Awkward Bowing II: Measures 19-20

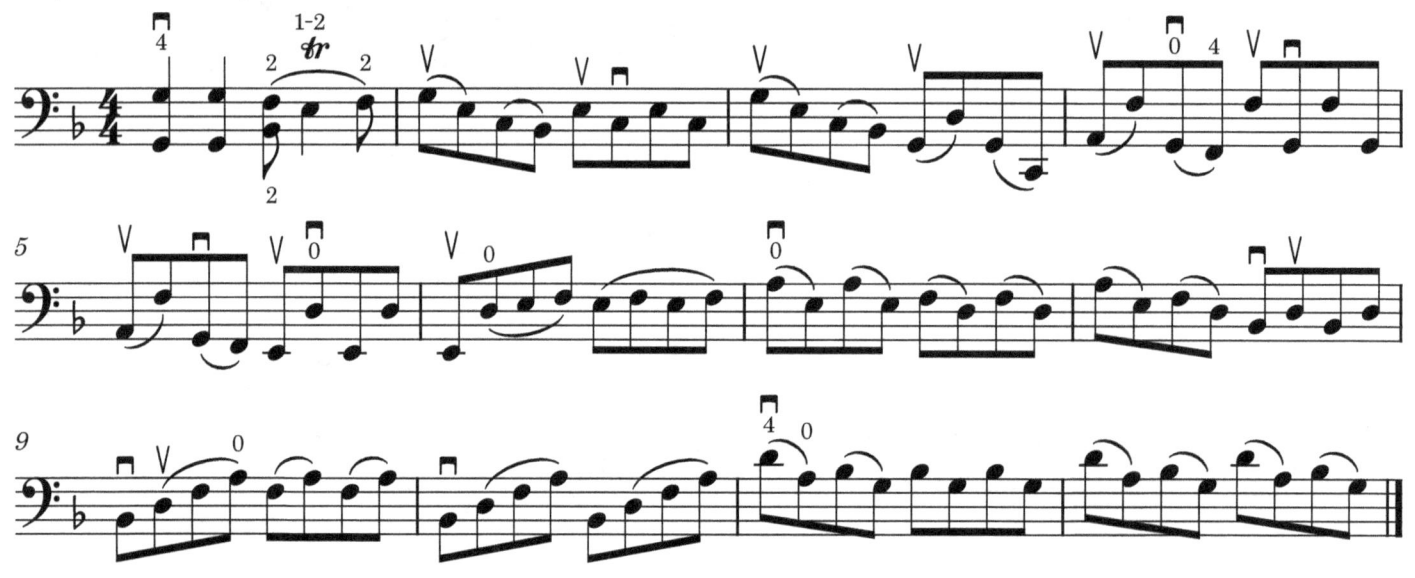

173. Shifting: Measures 19-20

The Bach Cello Suite No. 2 Study Book - Allemande 69

174. *Allemande, Part Six*: Measures 21-24 (end)

175. Learning the Shifts: Measure 21

©2026 C. Harvey Publications® All Rights Reserved.

176. Agility: Measure 22

177. Shifting I: Measure 22-23

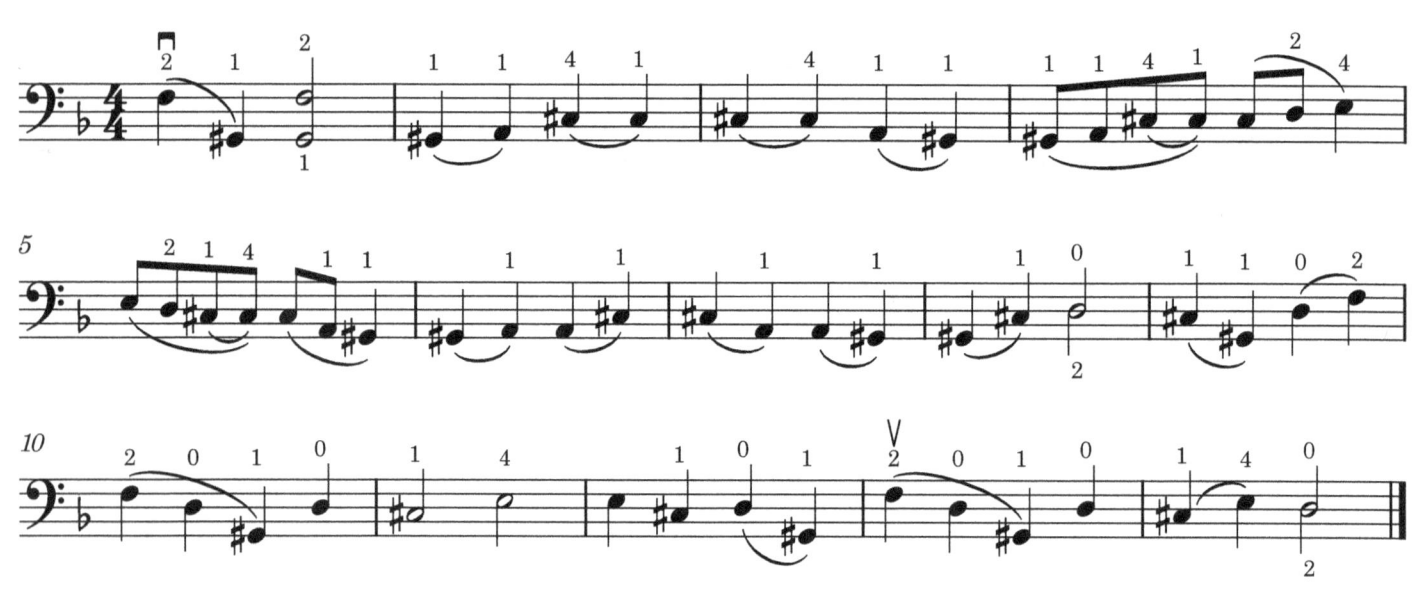

178. Shifting II: Measure 23

The Bach Cello Suite No. 2 Study Book - Allemande

179. Moving Across Strings in Positions: Measures 21-24

180. Bowing: Measures 21-24

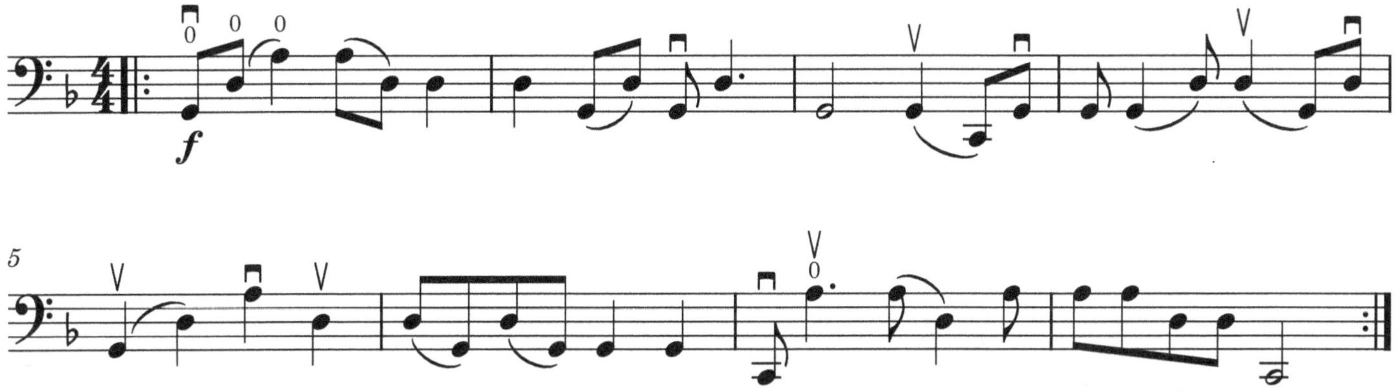

Repeat, getting faster each time.

The Bach Cello Suite No. 2 Study Book - Courante

181. *Courante, Part One*: Measures 1-6

182. Second Position: Measure 1

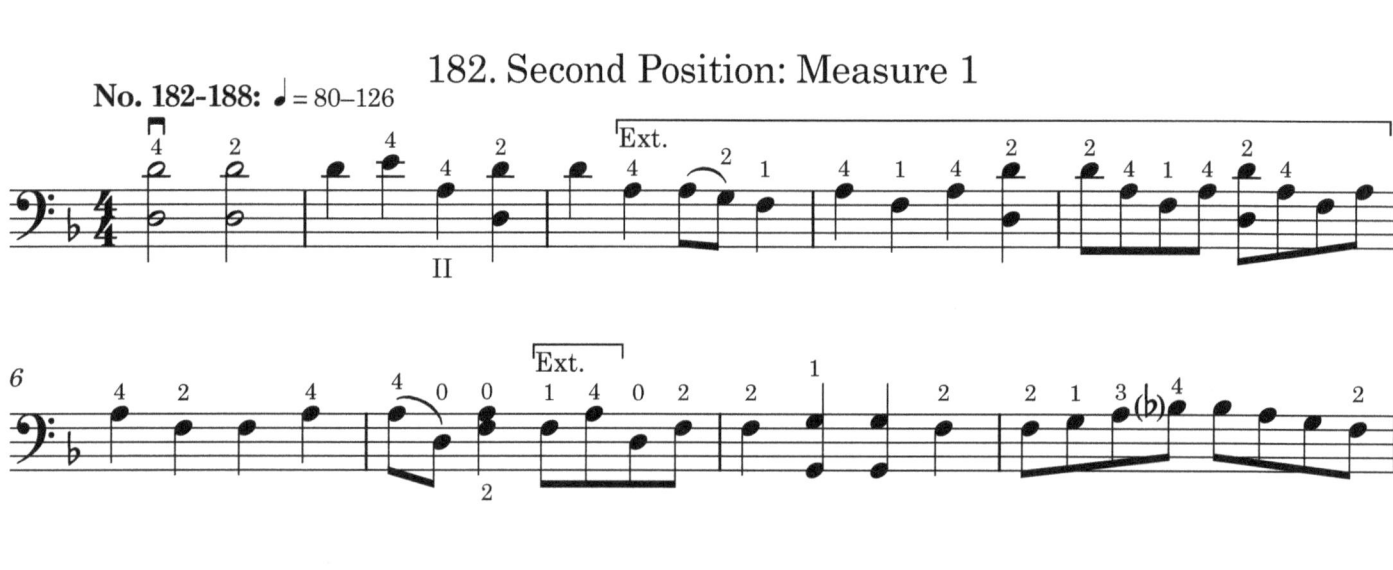

183. Chord Option 1, Downward Motion: Measure 2

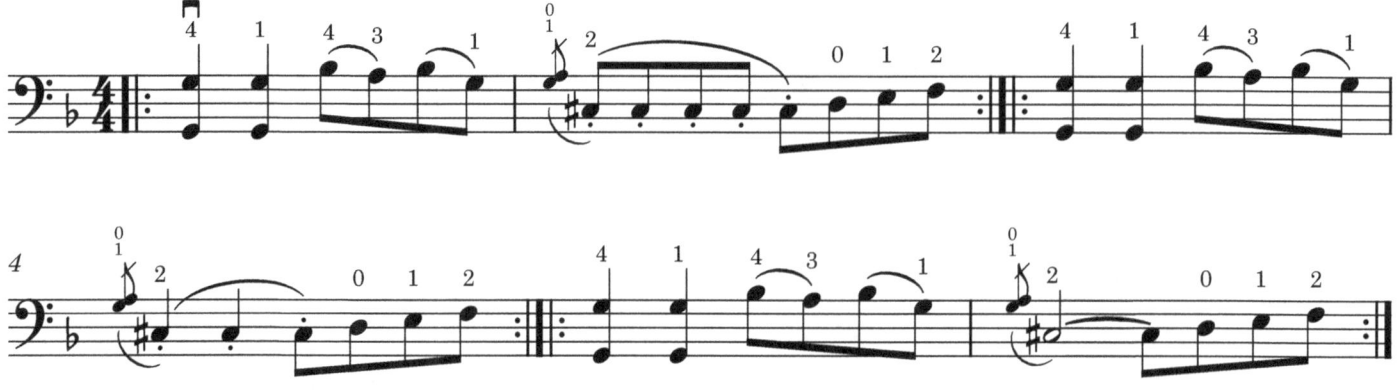

©2026 C. Harvey Publications® All Rights Reserved.

The Bach Cello Suite No. 2 Study Book - Courante

184. Chord Option 2, Upward Motion: Measure 2

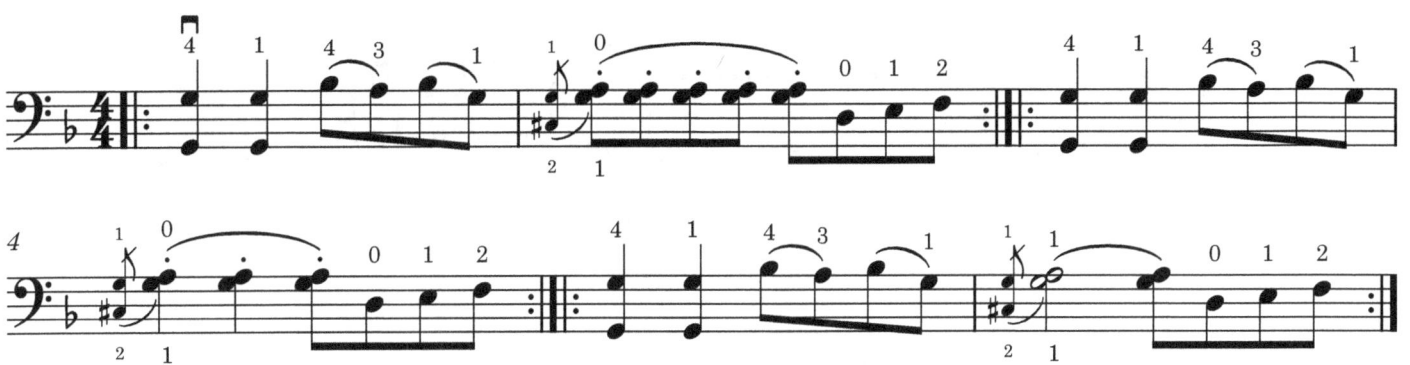

185. Chord Option 2, Up and Down: Measure 2

186. String Crossing and Second Position Shifting: Measures 2-3

187. Intonation: Measures 4-6

©2026 C. Harvey Publications® All Rights Reserved.

The Bach Cello Suite No. 2 Study Book - Courante

190. Chord: Measures 5-6

191. *Courante, Part Two*: Measures 7-12

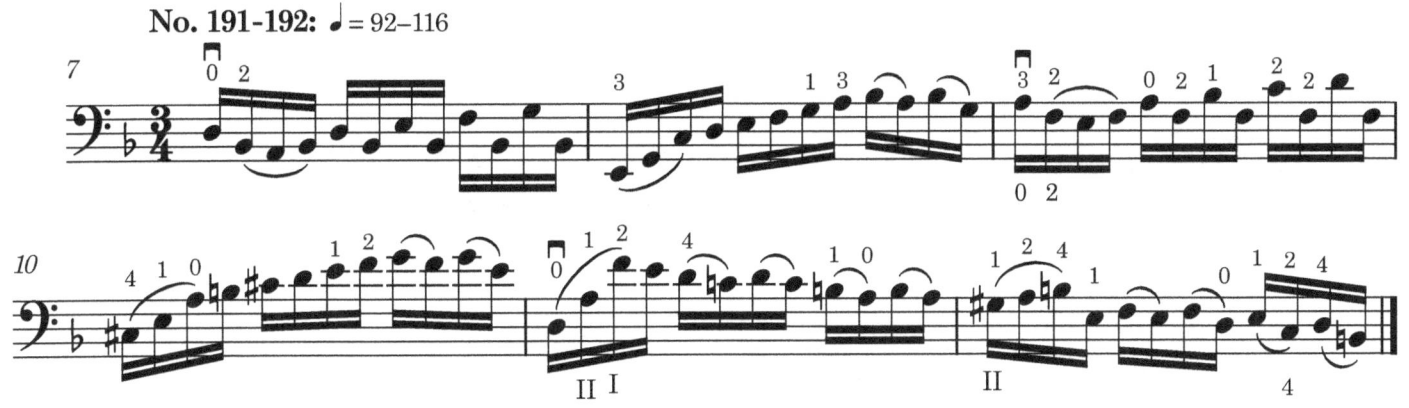

192. Bowing: Measures 7-12

©2026 C. Harvey Publications® All Rights Reserved.

193. Intonation: Measures 7-9

194. Fluency: Measures 7-10

195. Shifting to High Third Position: Measures 11-12

196. Shifting to Second Position Across Strings: Measure 12

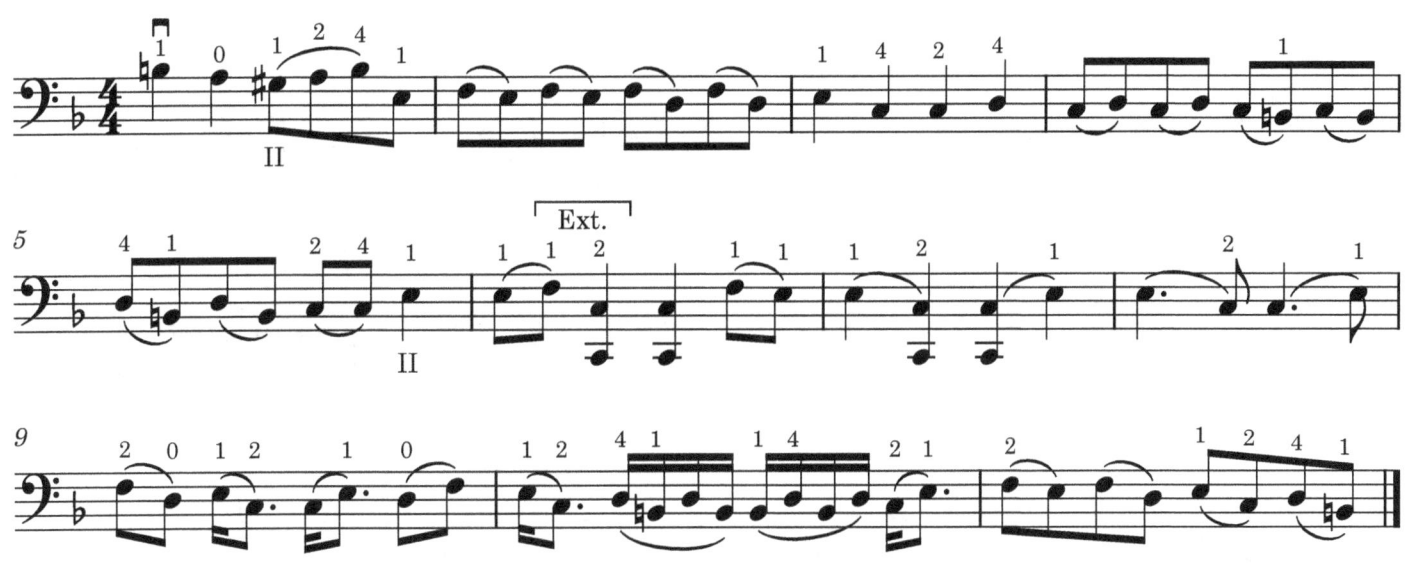

197. *Courante, Part Three*: Measures 13-16

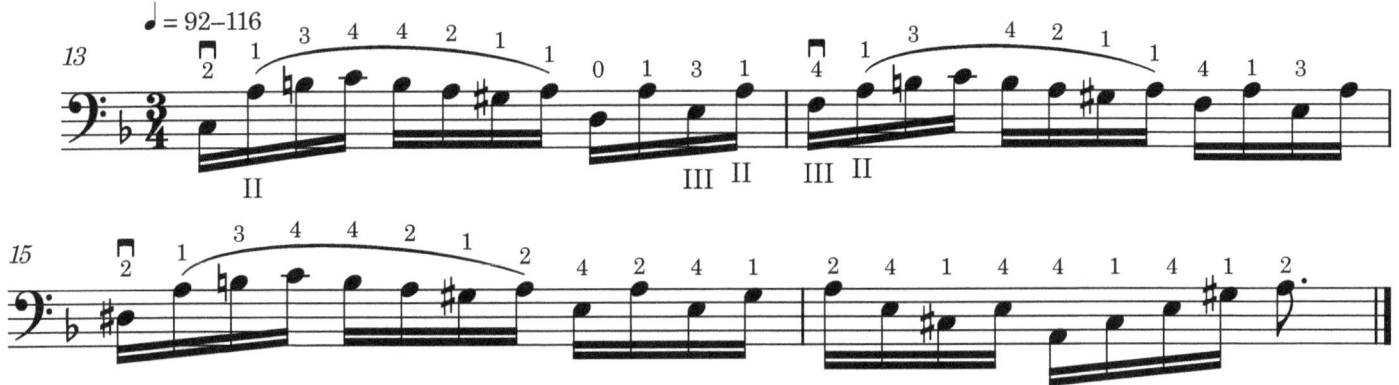

The Bach Cello Suite No. 2 Study Book - Courante

198. Bowing: Measures 13-16

199. Learning the Shifts: Measure 13-15

©2026 C. Harvey Publications® All Rights Reserved.

The Bach Cello Suite No. 2 Study Book - Courante

200. Learning the Shifts in Longer Slurs: Measures 13-16

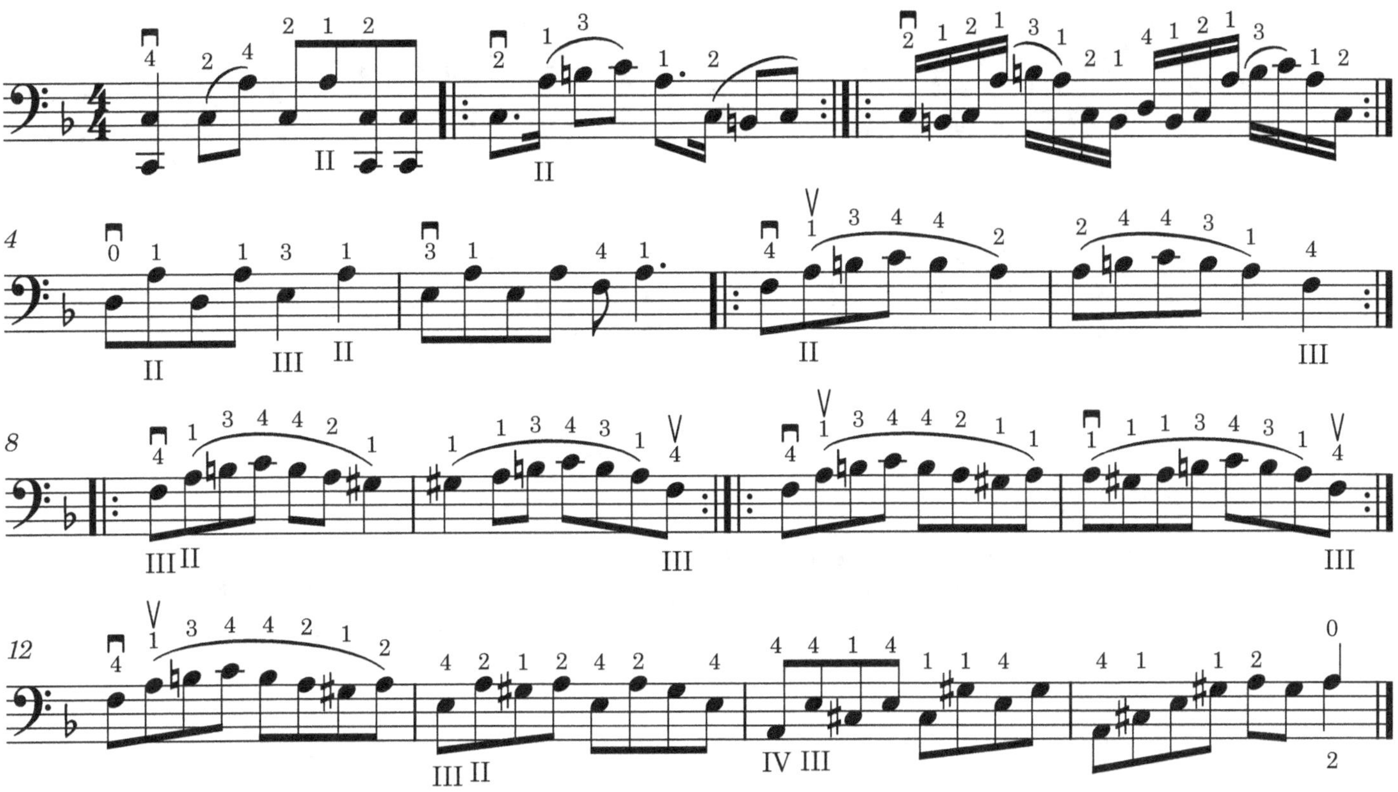

201. Fluency: Measures 13-16

* Pull bow quickly!

202. Recognizing the Patterns: Measures 13-16

©2026 C. Harvey Publications® All Rights Reserved.

203. *Courante, Part Four*: Measures 17-22

204. Shifting and Intonation: Measures 16-17

205. Mapping the Positions: Measures 17-18

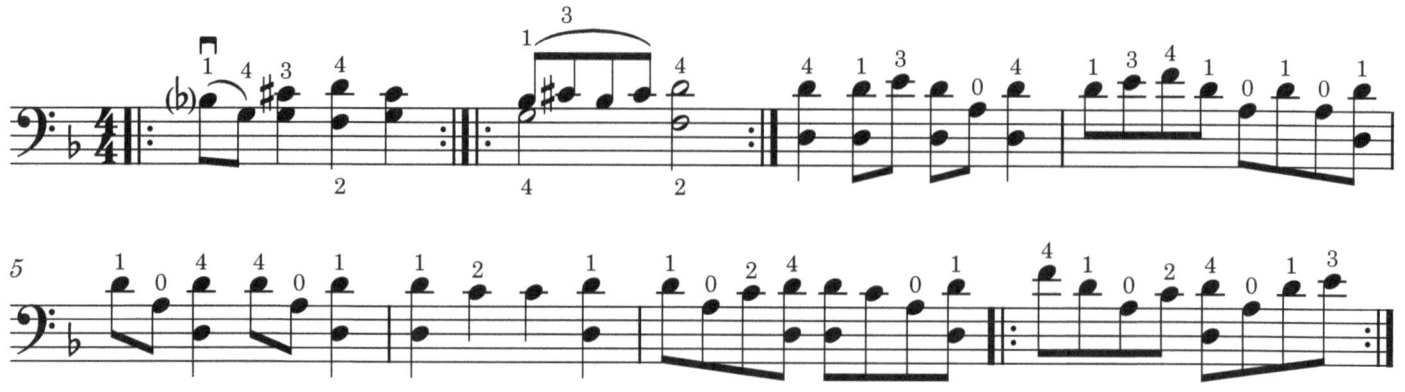

The Bach Cello Suite No. 2 Study Book - Courante 81

206. Left Hand Agility: Measures 17-19

207. Fluency: Measures 17-22

©2026 C. Harvey Publications® All Rights Reserved.

208. Bowing and Rhythm I: Measures 17-22

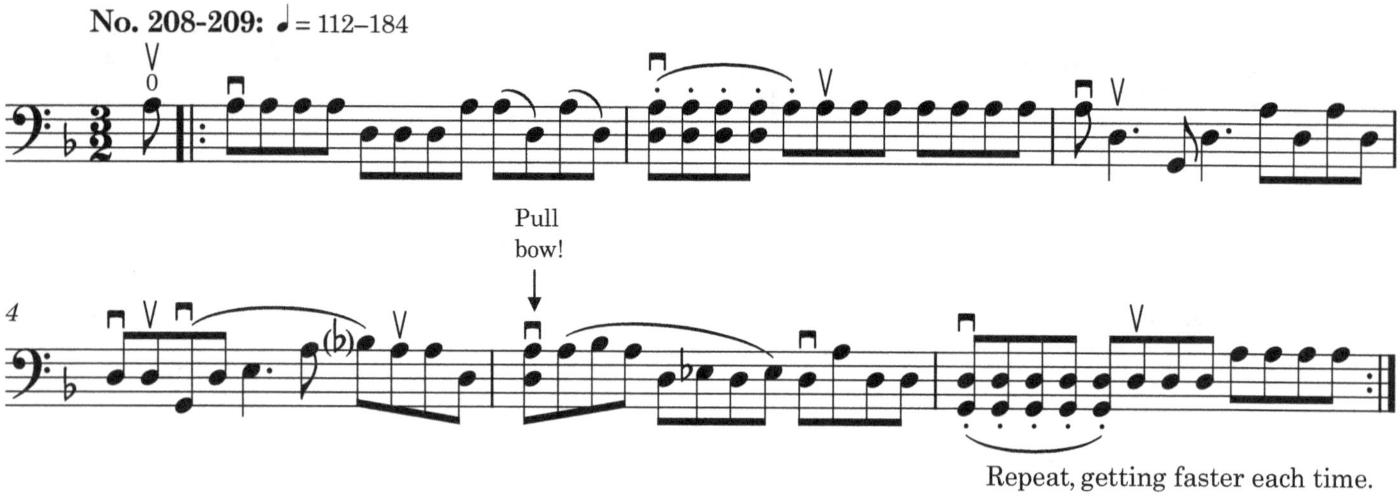

209. Bowing and Rhythm II: Measures 20-22

The Bach Cello Suite No. 2 Study Book - Courante

210. *Courante, Part Five*: Measures 23-28

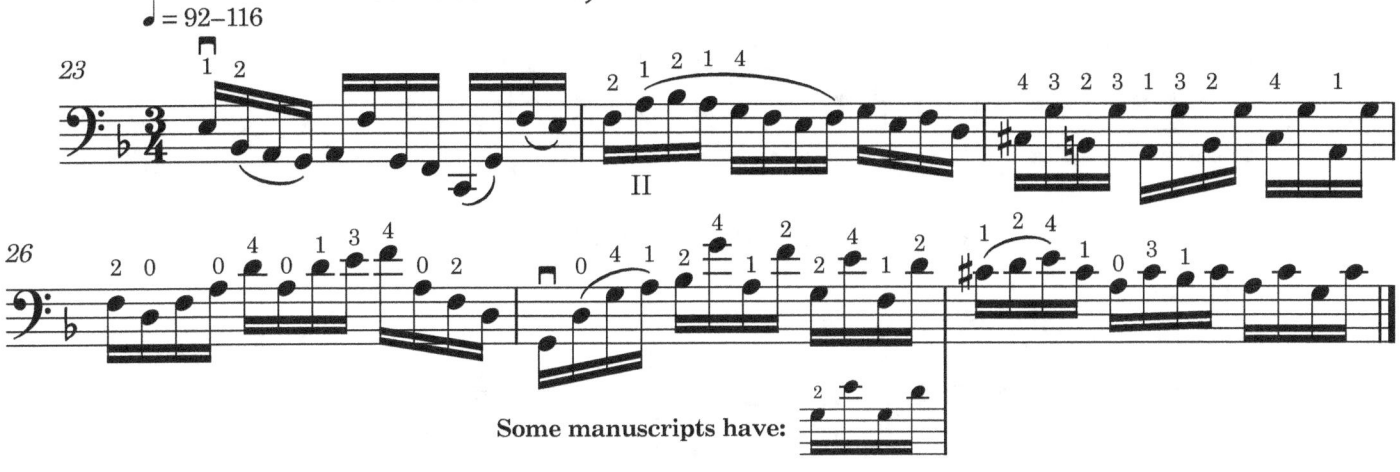

Some manuscripts have:

211. Bowing: Measures 23-28

Make sure this is smooth and completely **on** the string.

Repeat, getting faster each time.

212. Left-Hand Agility Across Strings: Measures 22-23

©2026 C. Harvey Publications® All Rights Reserved.

213. Bowing and Shifting: Measure 24

214. Learning the Notes: Measure 25

215. Intonation Across Strings: Measure 25

216. Open String Shifting: Measure 26

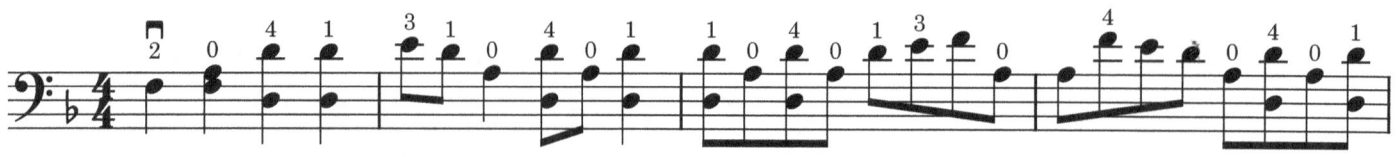

The Bach Cello Suite No. 2 Study Book - Courante

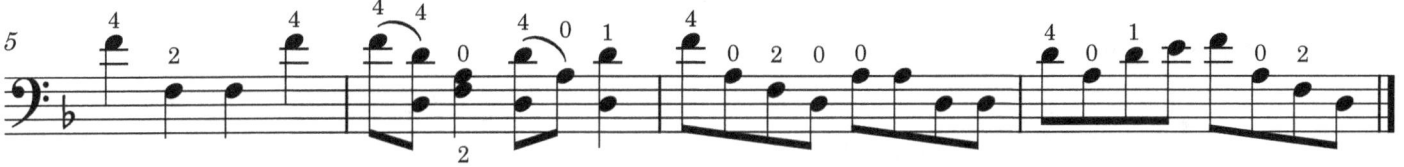

217. Backwards Broken Sixths: Measure 27

218. Extended and Closed Positions: Measures 27-28

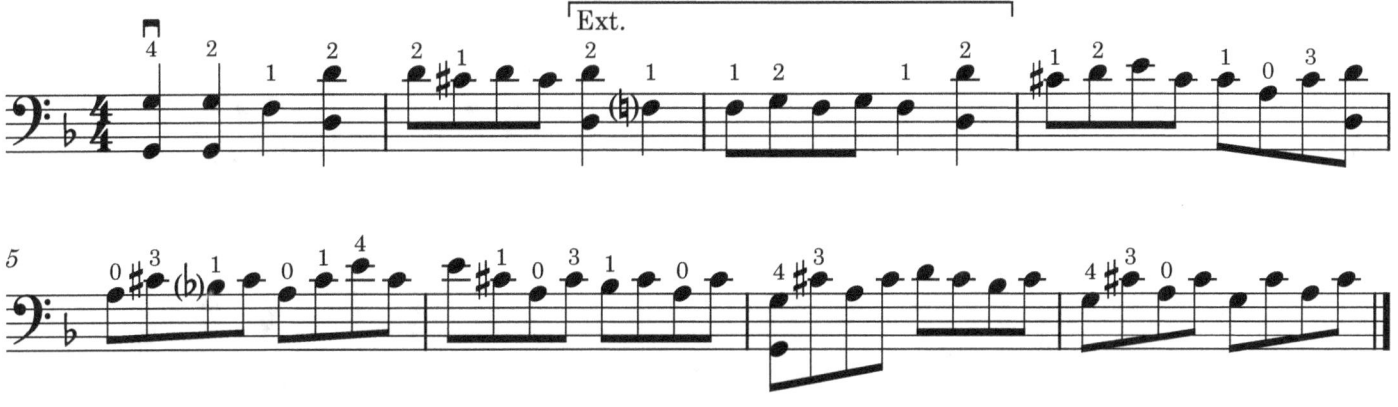

219. *Courante, Part Six*: Measures 29-32 (end)

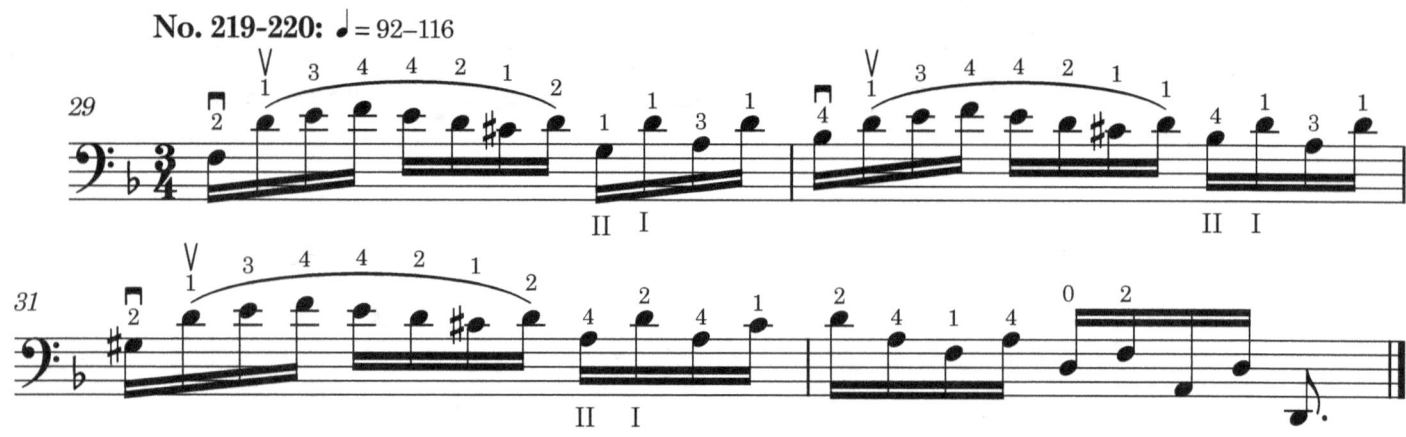

220. String Crossing: Measures 29-32

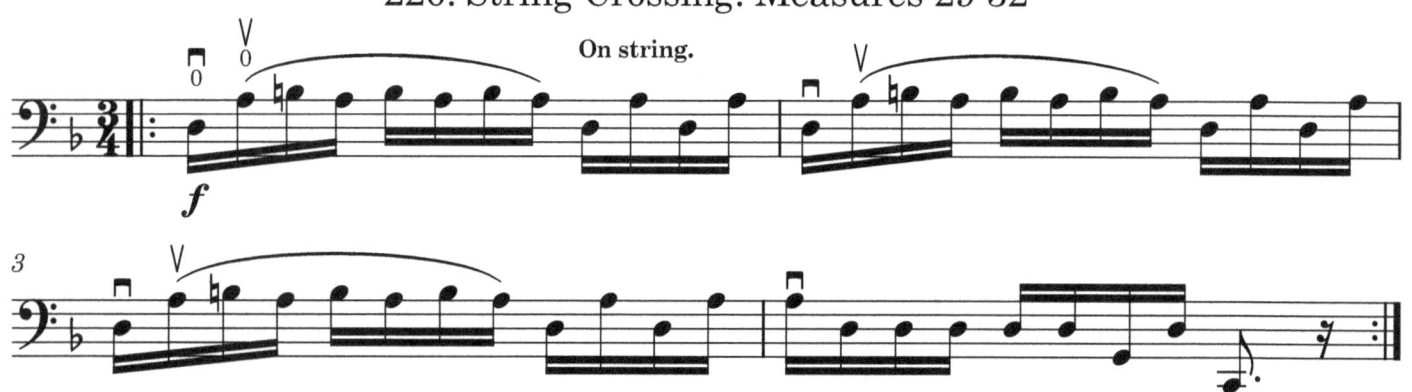

221. Shifting Between Third and Second Position: Measures 29-31

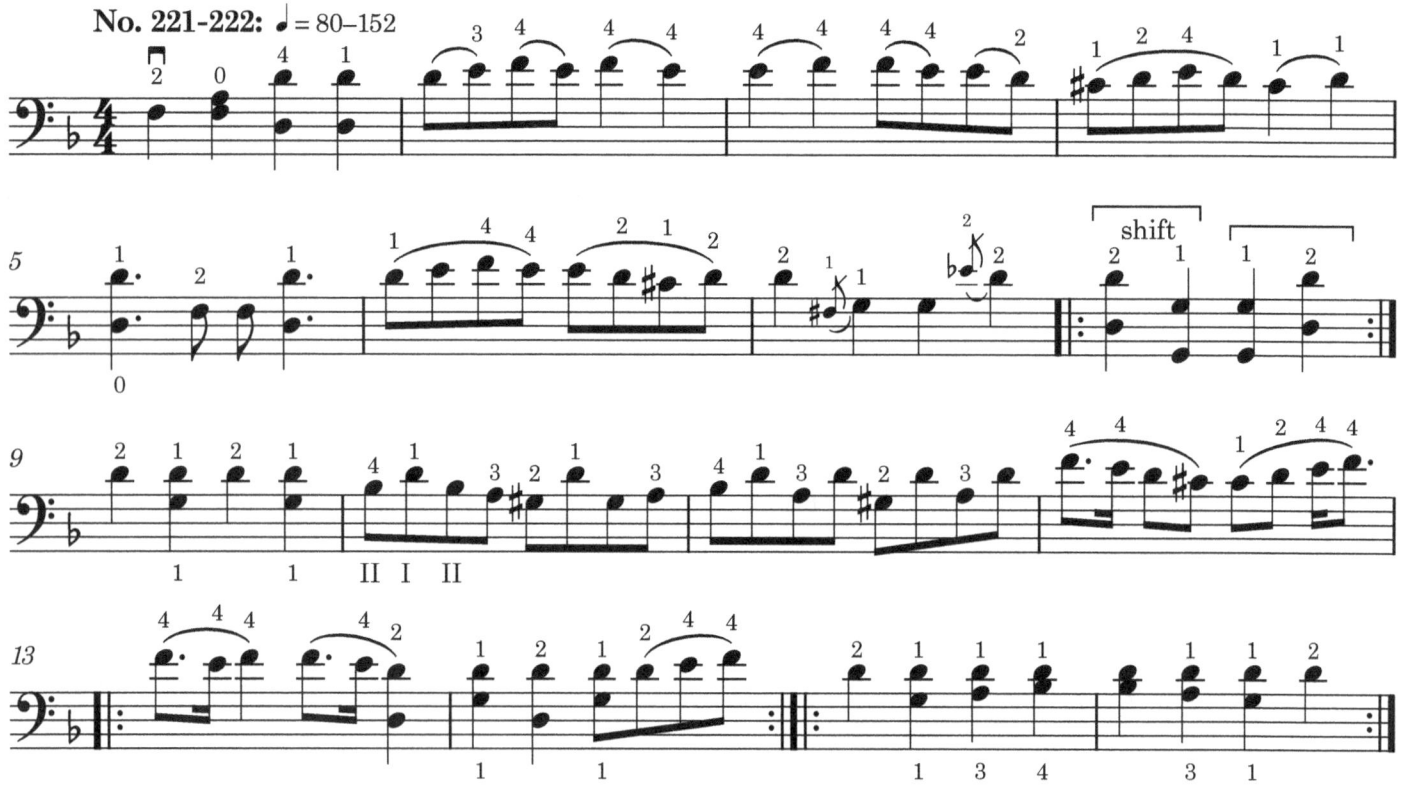

The Bach Cello Suite No. 2 Study Book - Courante

224. *Sarabande, Part One*: Measures 1-6

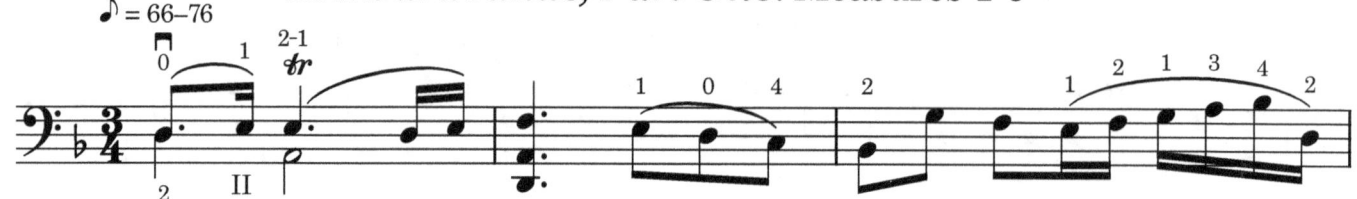

Note: Vibrato may be used on all exercises once the notes are in tune.

225. Learning the Trill: Measure 1

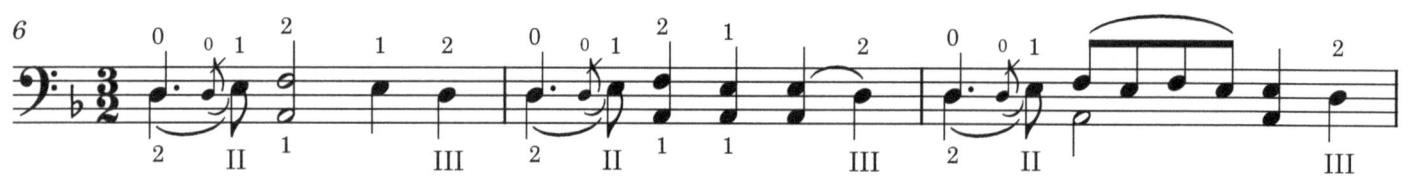

The Bach Cello Suite No. 2 Study Book - Sarabande

226. Intonation and Shifting: Measures 1-3

227. Shifting: Measures 3-4

"Contract" the hand by picking up the 3rd finger so that 2nd finger can be next to the 4th finger.

228. Shifts and a Trill: Measures 3-4

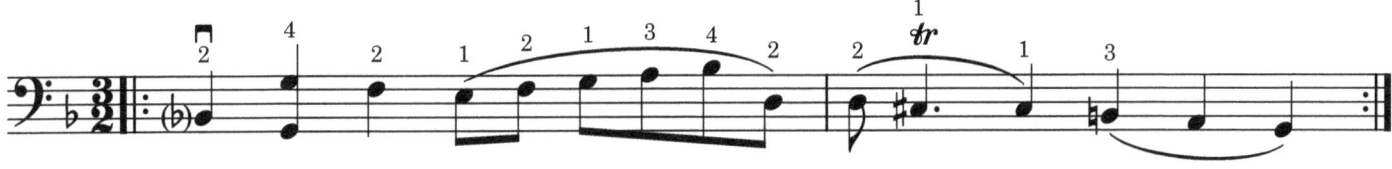

©2026 C. Harvey Publications® All Rights Reserved.

229. Intonation: Measures 3-4

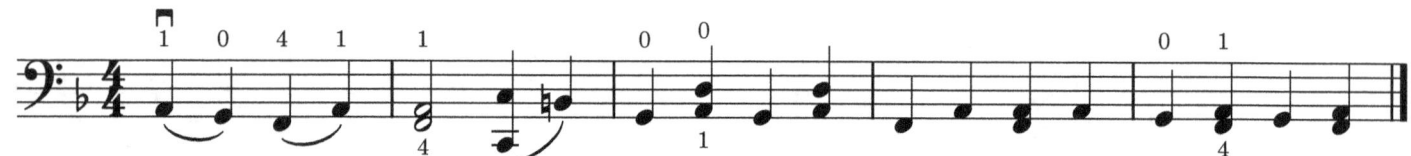

230. Fluency: Measures 1-6

231. *Sarabande, Part Two*: Measures 7-12

No. 232-240: ♩ = 66–76 ### 232. Learning the Shifts: Measure 7

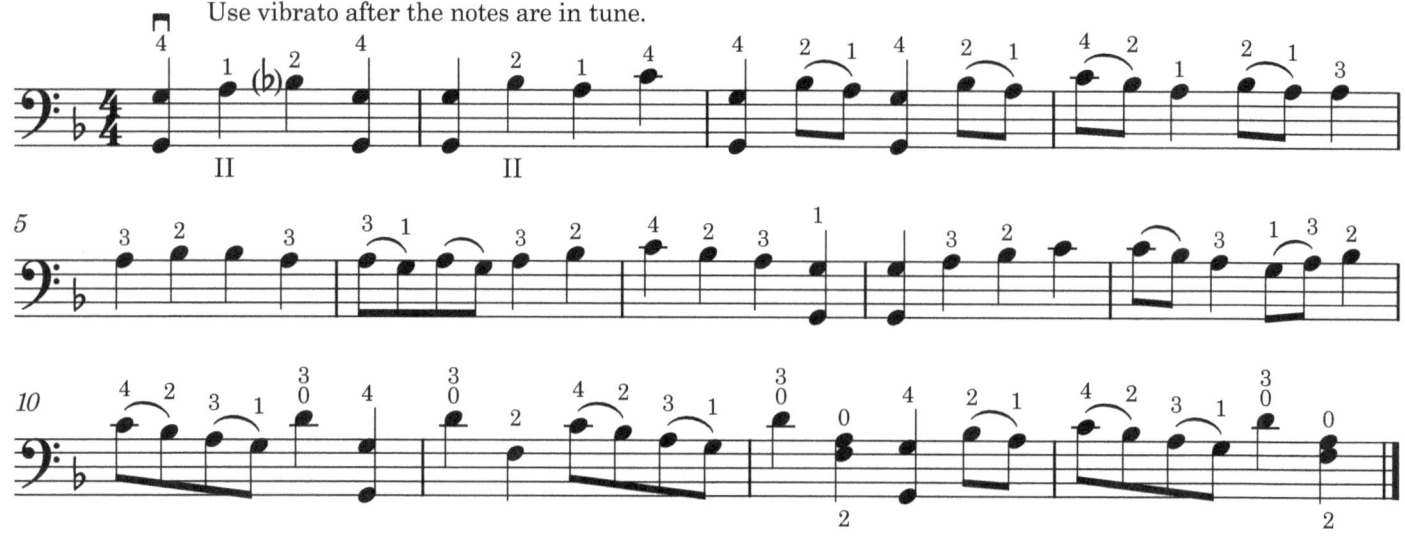

The Bach Cello Suite No. 2 Study Book - Sarabande

233. Connections: Measures 7-9

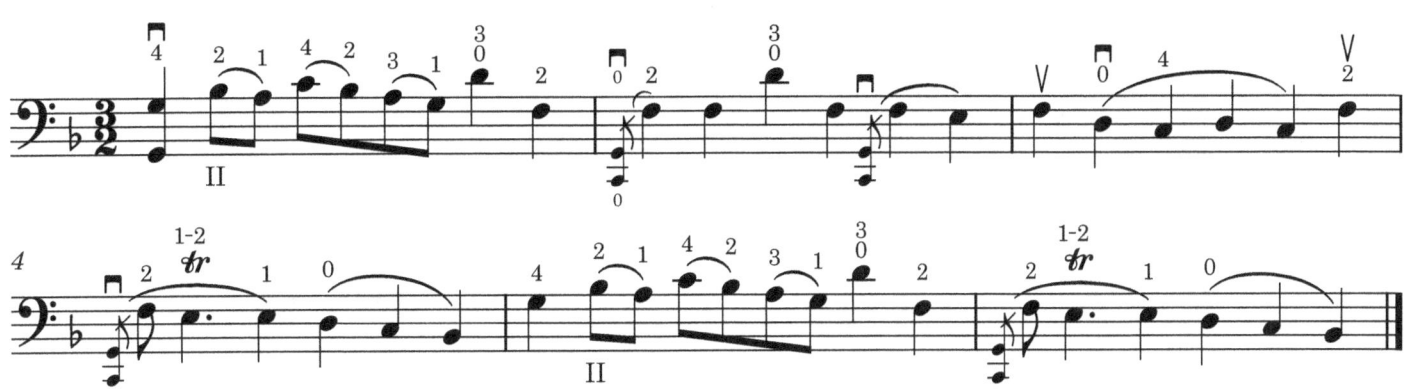

234. Shifting and Extending Across Strings: Measure 9

235. Connections Across Strings: Measures 8-9

©2026 C. Harvey Publications® All Rights Reserved.

236. Moving Between Half and First Position: Measures 9-10

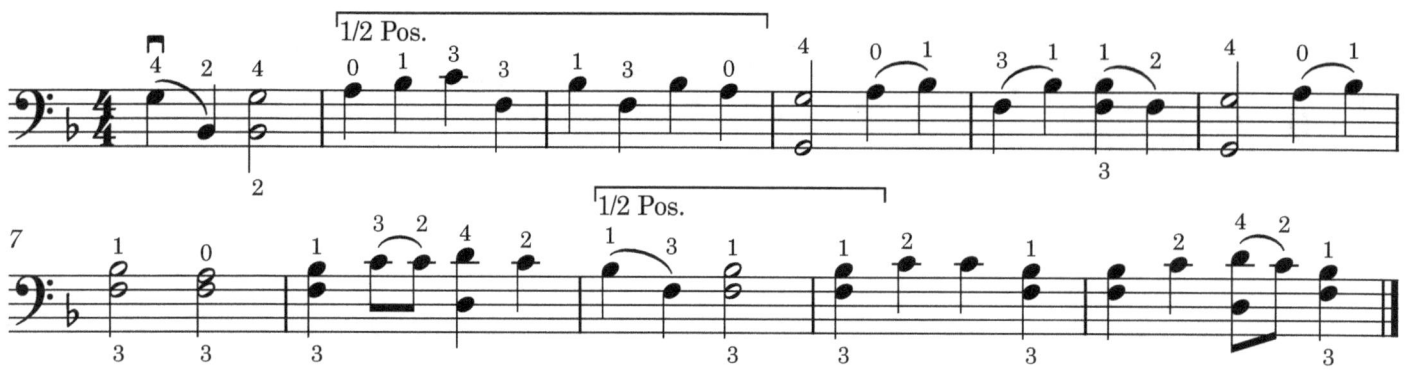

237. Moving Between Positions: Measures 9-11

238. Bowing and Tone: Measures 7-12

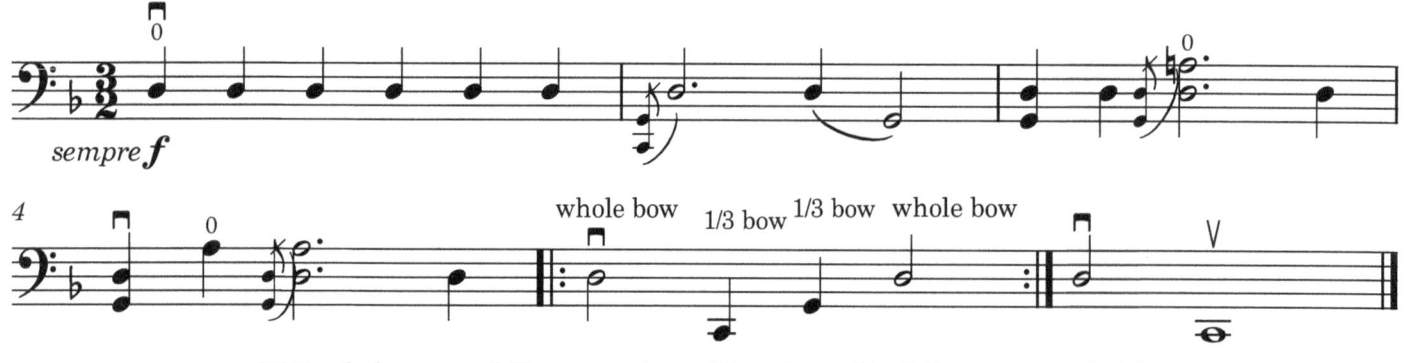

239. Advanced Intonation (Optional): Measures 9-12

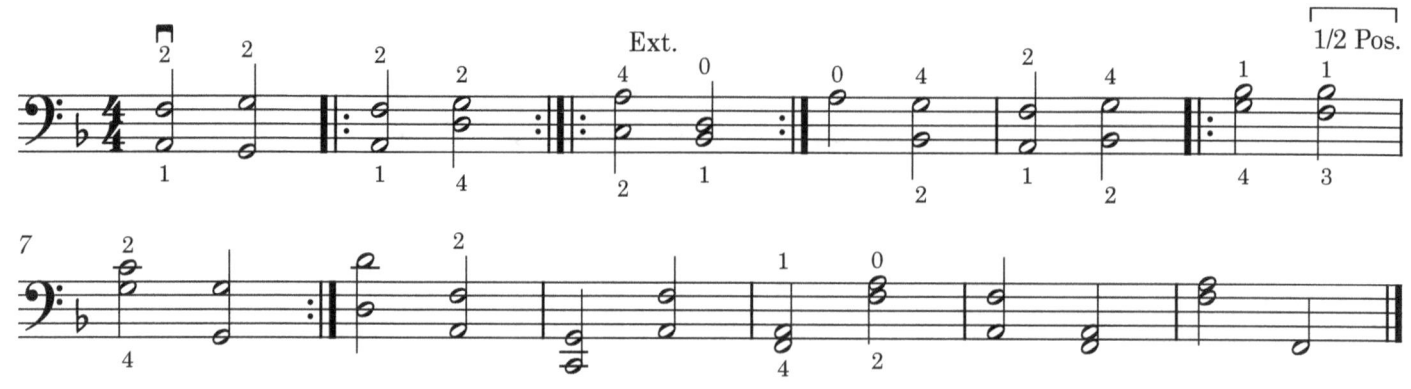

The Bach Cello Suite No. 2 Study Book - Sarabande

240. Fluency: Measures 7-12

241. *Sarabande, Part Three*: Measures 13-20

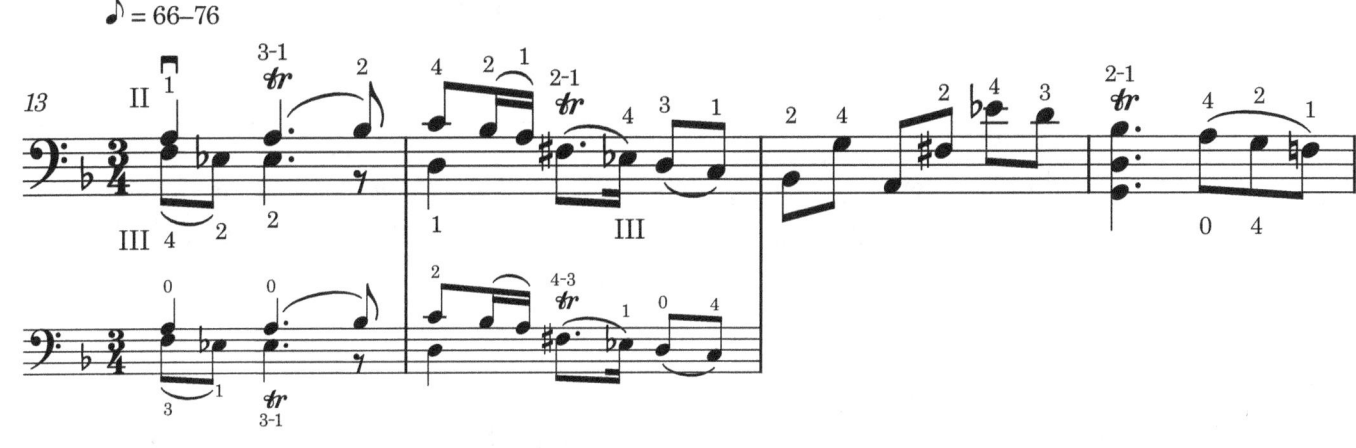

242. Playing Across Strings With Different Fingers: Measures 12-13

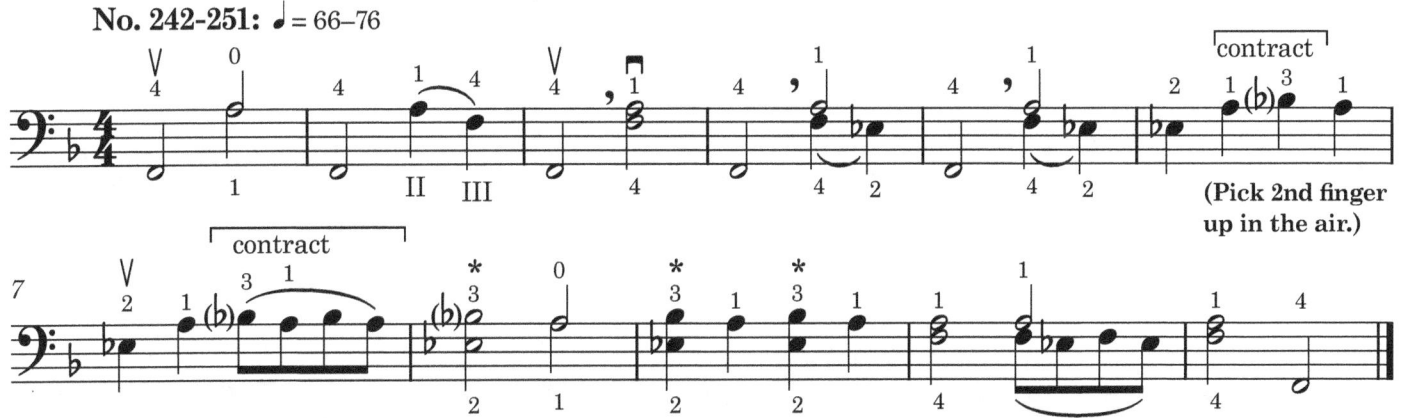

*Note: 3rd and 2nd finger are directly across from each other, across strings. Fingernails should face bridge.

©2026 C. Harvey Publications® All Rights Reserved.

243. Working on Playing Across Strings: Measure 13

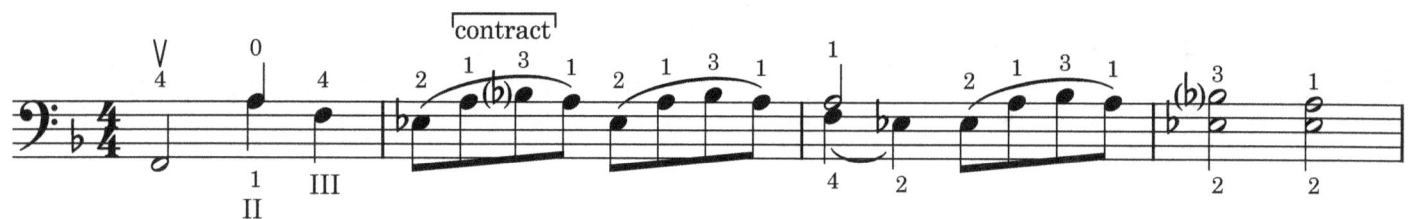

244. Left Hand Agility: Measure 13

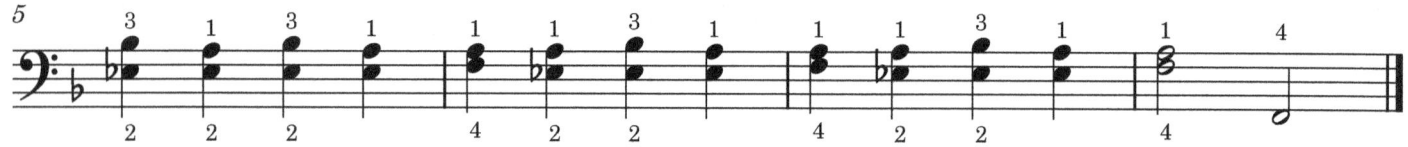

The Bach Cello Suite No. 2 Study Book - Sarabande

245. Shifting Backwards and Across Strings: Measure 14

246. Shifting to a Trill and Shifting Across Strings: Measures 14-15

247. Extended and Closed First Position: Measure 15

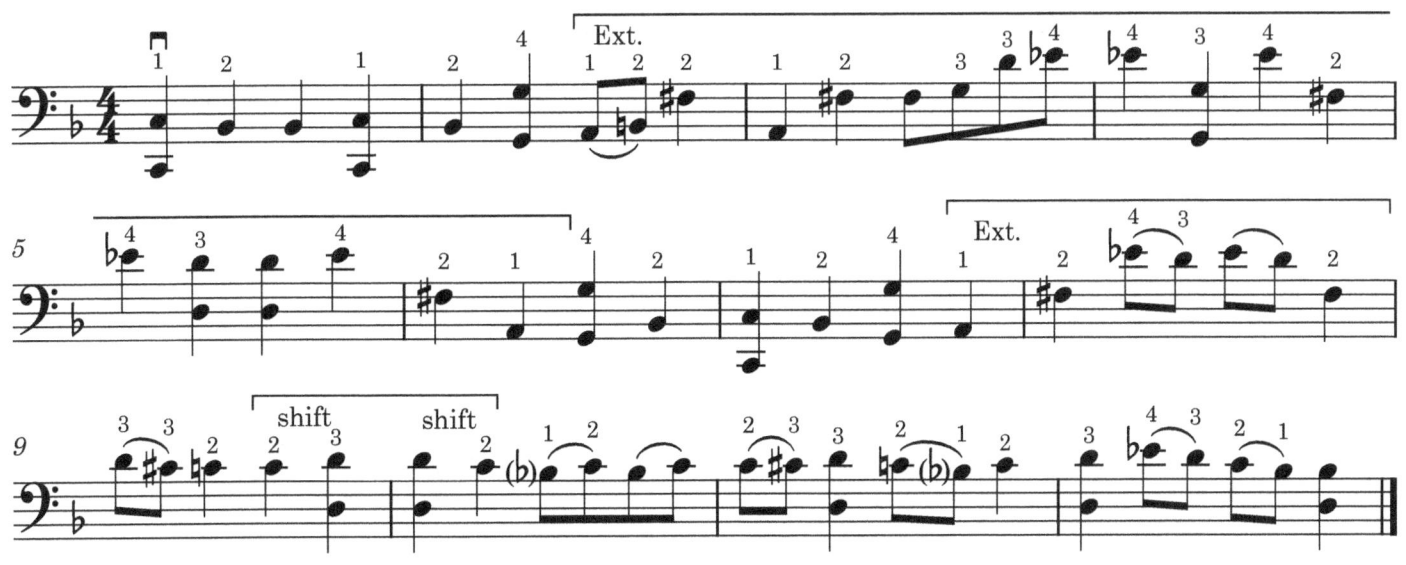

©2026 C. Harvey Publications® All Rights Reserved.

248. Fingering Option No. 1, Contortions: Measures 13-14

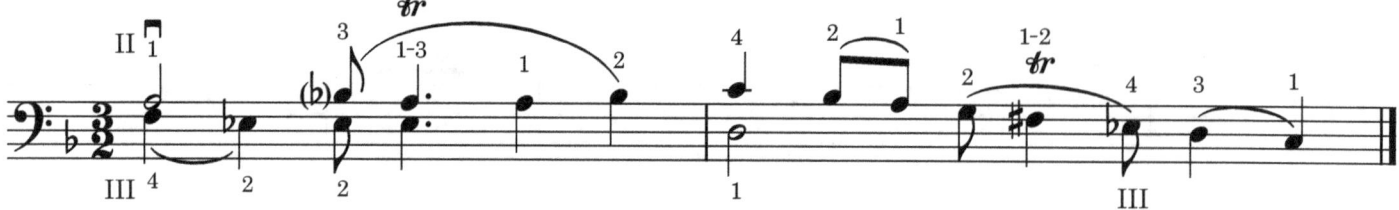

249. Fingering Option No. 2, Using Half Position: Measures 13-14

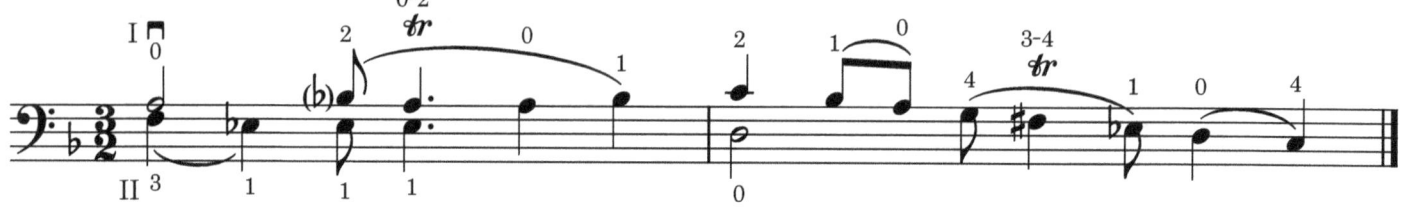

Author's note: Option 2 did not work for my hands but some hands may like it better.

250. Fingering Option No. 3, Trill on E-Flat: Measures 13-14

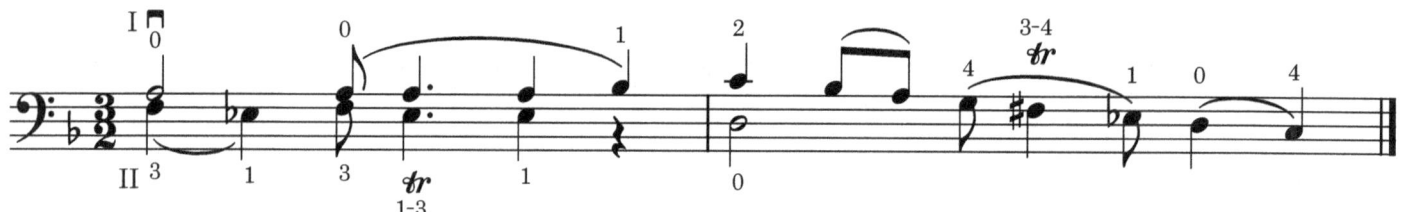

251. Fingering Option No. 4, Practical and Musical: Measures 13-14

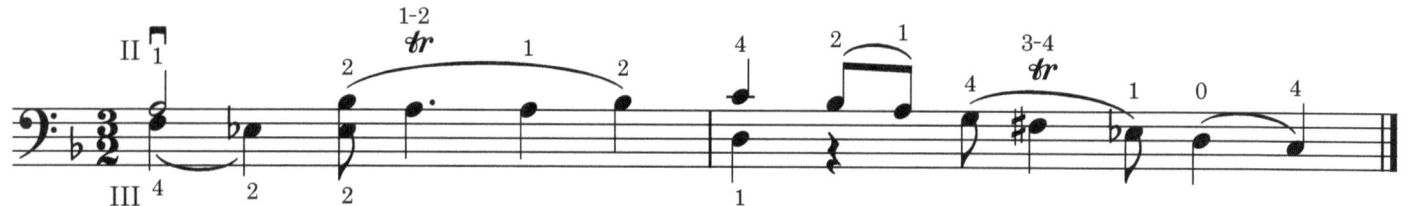

Author's note: Option 4 is the fingering and style used by a majority of performances and recordings and this is the one I like the best! Simple and effective.

252. How This is Typically Played: Measure 14

The Bach Cello Suite No. 2 Study Book - Sarabande 97

253. Shifting to Second Position Across Strings: Measures 15-16

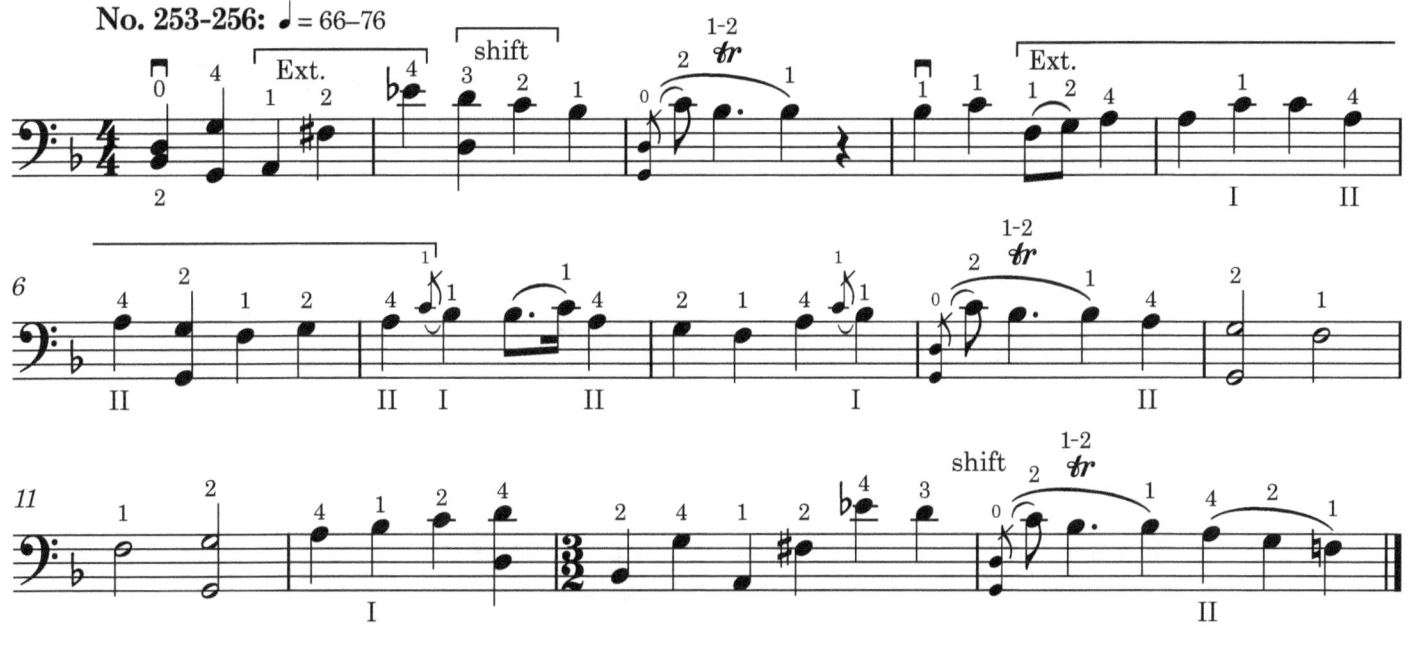

254. Learning the Notes: Measures 17-18

255. Shifting to Third Position: Measures 18-19

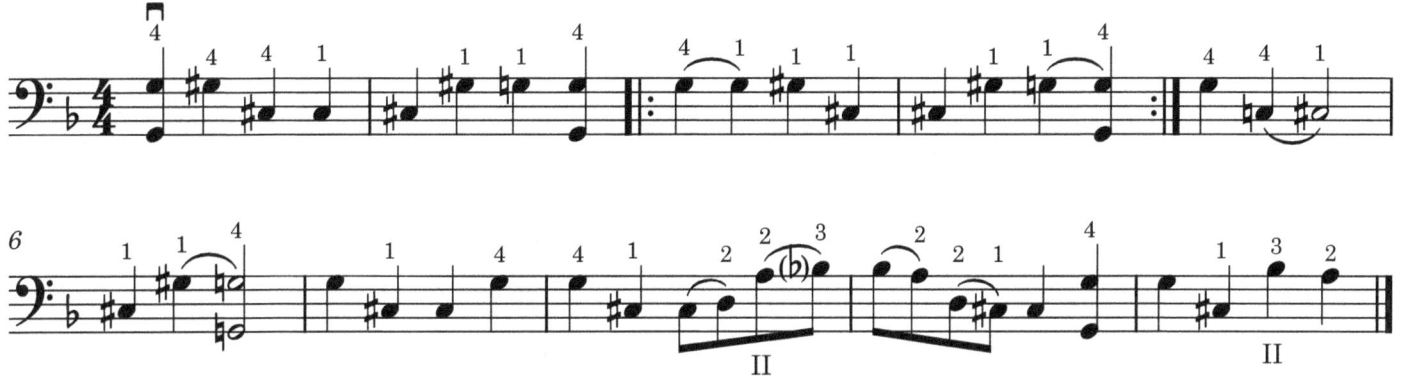

©2026 C. Harvey Publications® All Rights Reserved.

256. String Crossing and Shifting: Measures 19-20

257. *Sarabande, Part Four*: Measures 21-28 (end)

Optional bowing for first time through, before the repeat.

The Bach Cello Suite No. 2 Study Book - Sarabande

258. Connections: Measures 21-23

259. Switching Fingers: Measure 23

260. Fluency: Measures 21-23

261. Shifting to Second Position Across Strings: Measures 23-24

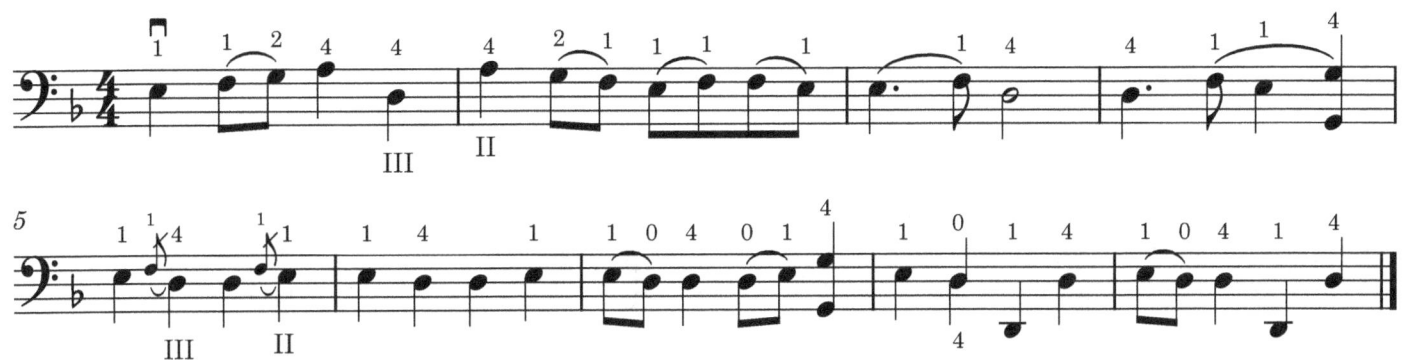

©2026 C. Harvey Publications® All Rights Reserved.

The Bach Cello Suite No. 2 Study Book - Sarabande   101

265. "Hooked" Bowing: Measures 25-26

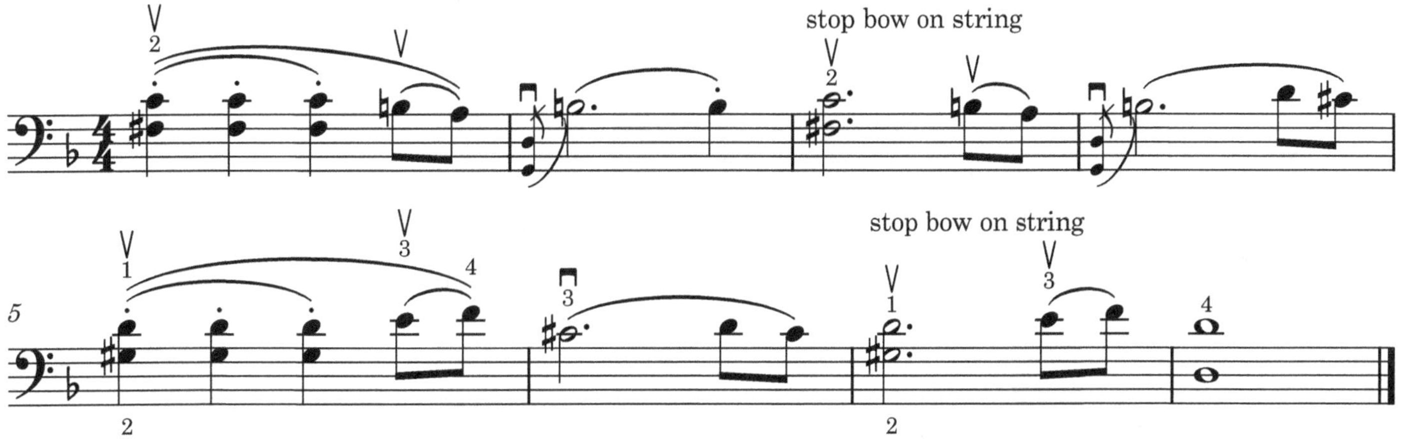

266. Rhythm and Bowing: Measures 25-28

267. Fluency: Measures 20-28

* Note: This is how measure 25 is typically played.

©2026 C. Harvey Publications® All Rights Reserved.

268. *Menuet I, Part One, Fingering 1*: Measures 1-8

269. Reaching the Chord: Measure 1, *Fingering 1*

270. Extensions and Intonation: Measure 1, *Fingering 1*

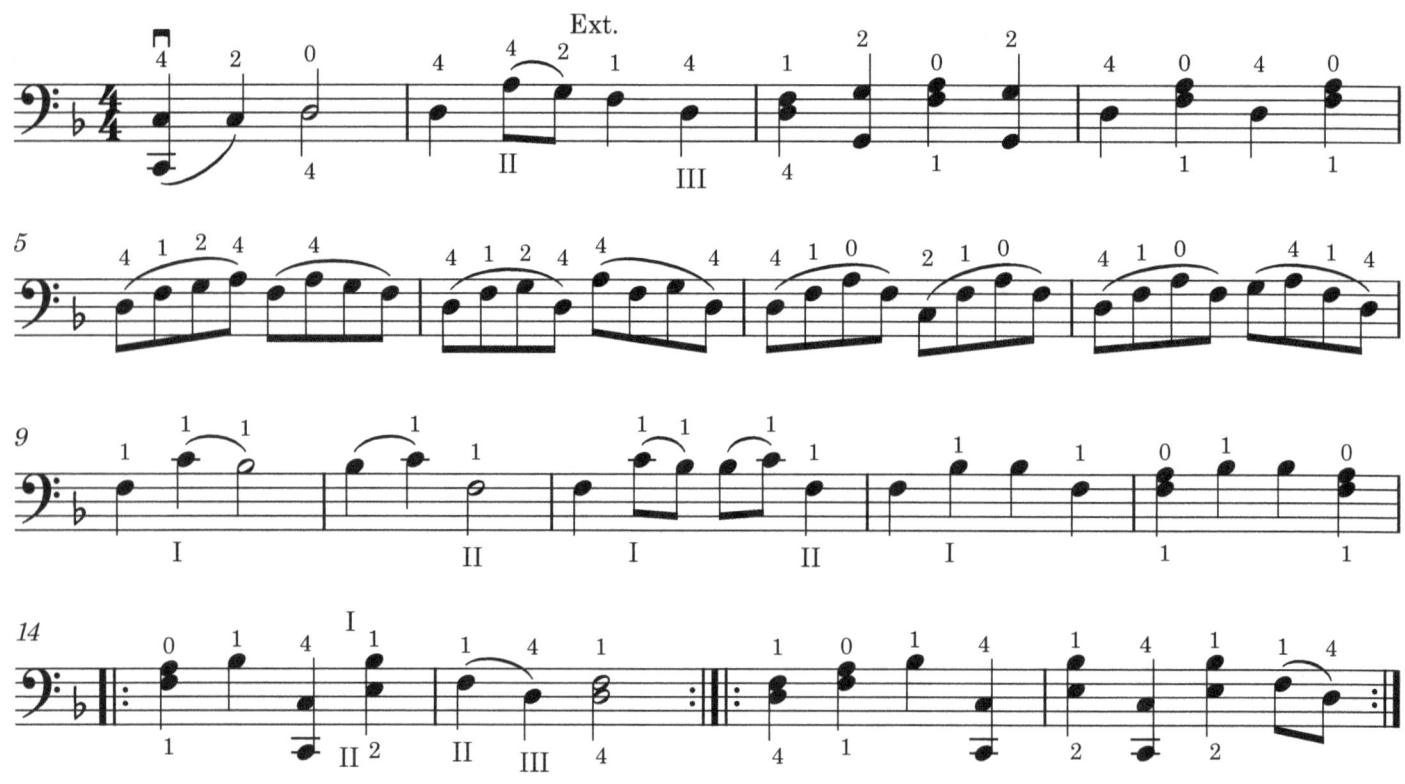

The Bach Cello Suite No. 2 Study Book - Menuet I

271. Chord: Measures 1-2, *Fingering 1*

272. Agility in Double Stops: Measures 1-3, *Fingering 1*

273. *Menuet I, Part One, Fingering 2*: Measures 1-8

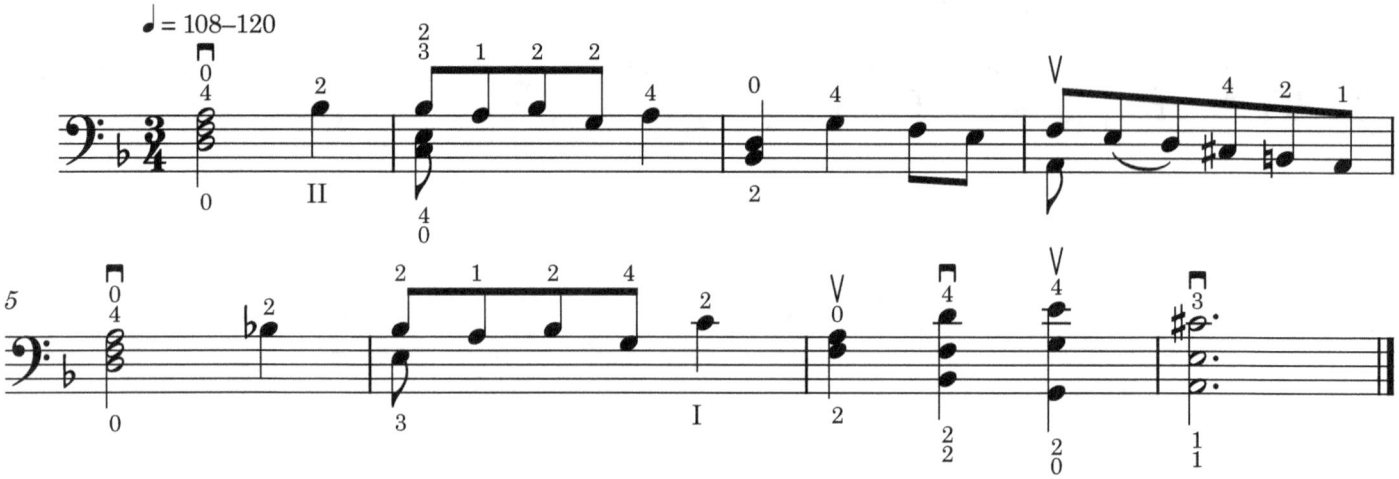

274. The Chord Across Strings in Fourth Position: Measure 1, *Fingering 2*

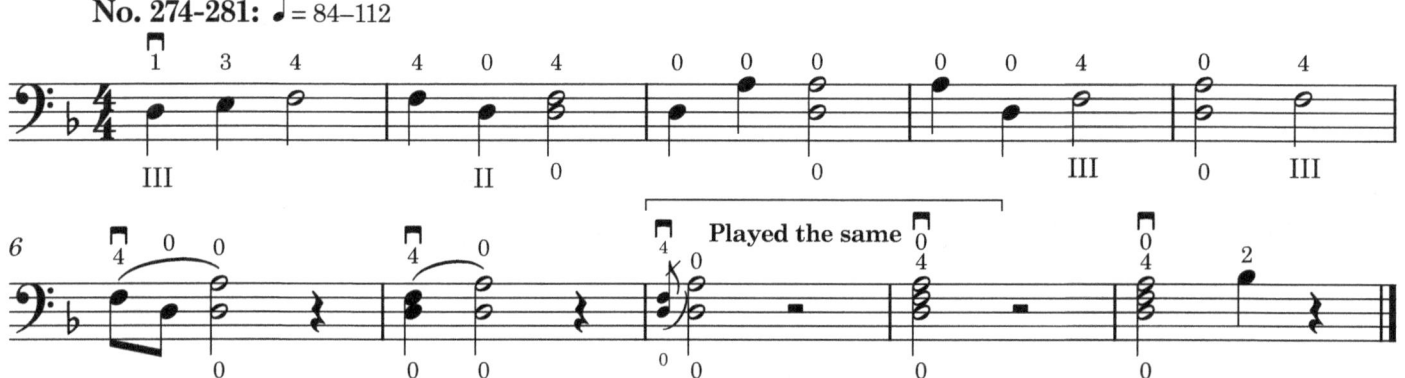

275. Finding the Notes After the Harmonic: Measures 1-2, *Fingering 2*

©2026 C. Harvey Publications® All Rights Reserved.

The Bach Cello Suite No. 2 Study Book - Menuet I 105

276. Transitions: Measures 1-2, *Fingering 2*

277. Landing on Two Strings at Once: Measures 1-3, *Fingering 2*

©2026 C. Harvey Publications® All Rights Reserved.

278. Switching Fingers Across Strings: Measures 3-4, *Both Fingerings*

279. Shifting To and From the Chord: Measures 4-6, *Fingering 1*

The Bach Cello Suite No. 2 Study Book - Menuet I 107

280. Shifting To and From the Chord: Measures 4-6, *Fingering 2*

281. Chords: Measures 6-9, *Both Fingerings*

©2026 C. Harvey Publications® All Rights Reserved.

282. *Menuet I, Part Two*: Measures 9-18

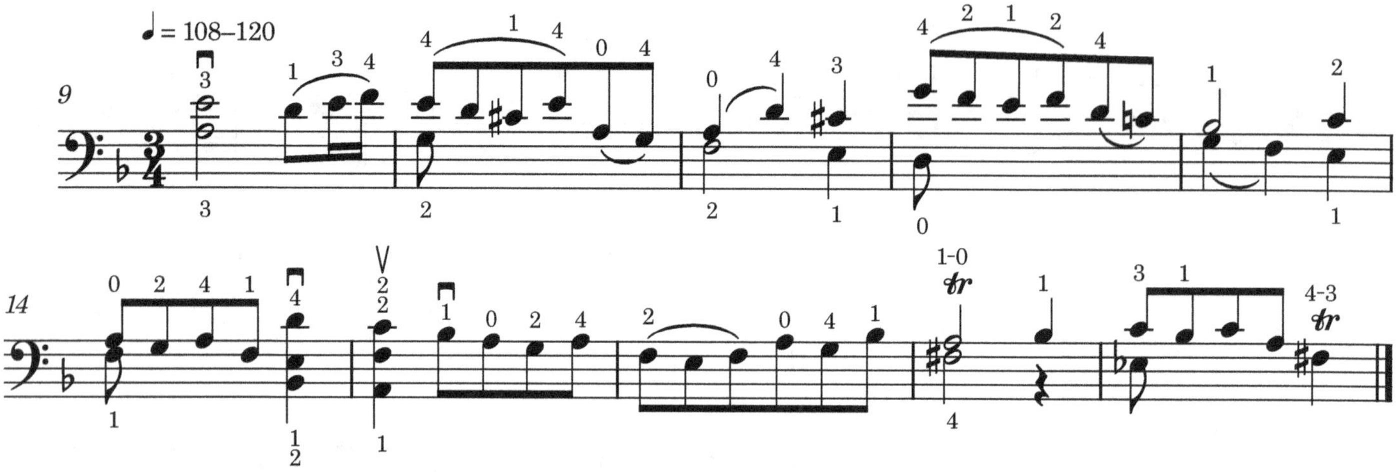

283. Learning the Notes: Measures 8-12

The Bach Cello Suite No. 2 Study Book - Menuet I   109

284. Intonation: Measures 9-12

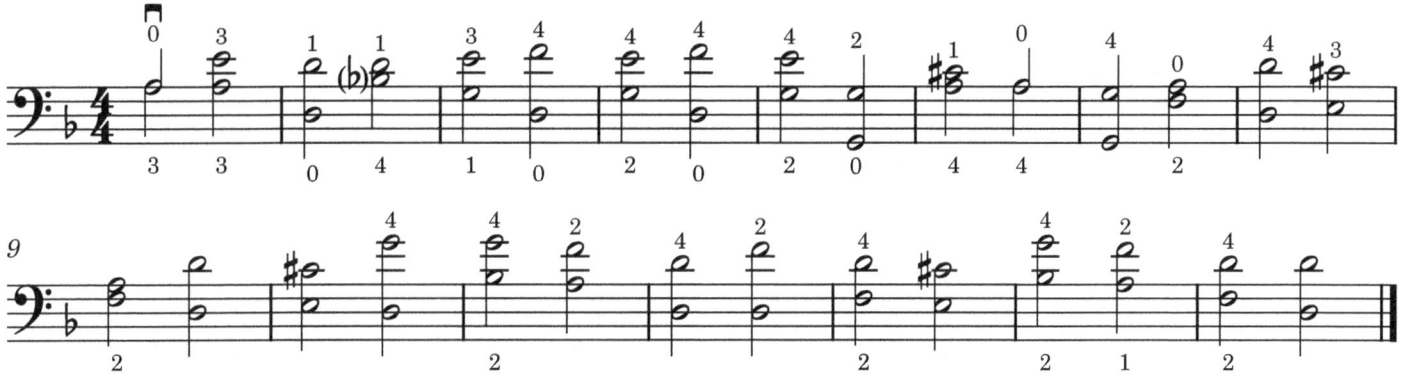

285. Extending in Double Stops: Measures 12-13

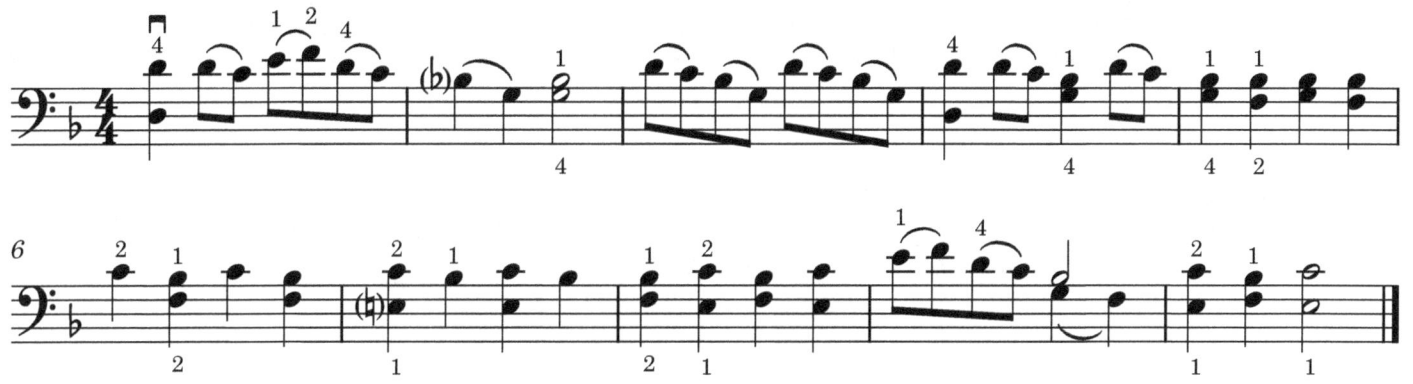

286. Shifting: Measures 13-15

©2026 C. Harvey Publications® All Rights Reserved.

287. Learning the Connections: Measures 14-17

288. Moving In and Out of the Trills: Measures 16-18

The Bach Cello Suite No. 2 Study Book - Menuet I 111

289. *Menuet I, Part Three*: Measures 19-24 (end)

290. Chords: Measures 18-19

©2026 C. Harvey Publications® All Rights Reserved.

291. Second Position Double Stops: Measures 20-21

292. Closed and Extended Second Position: Measures 21-22

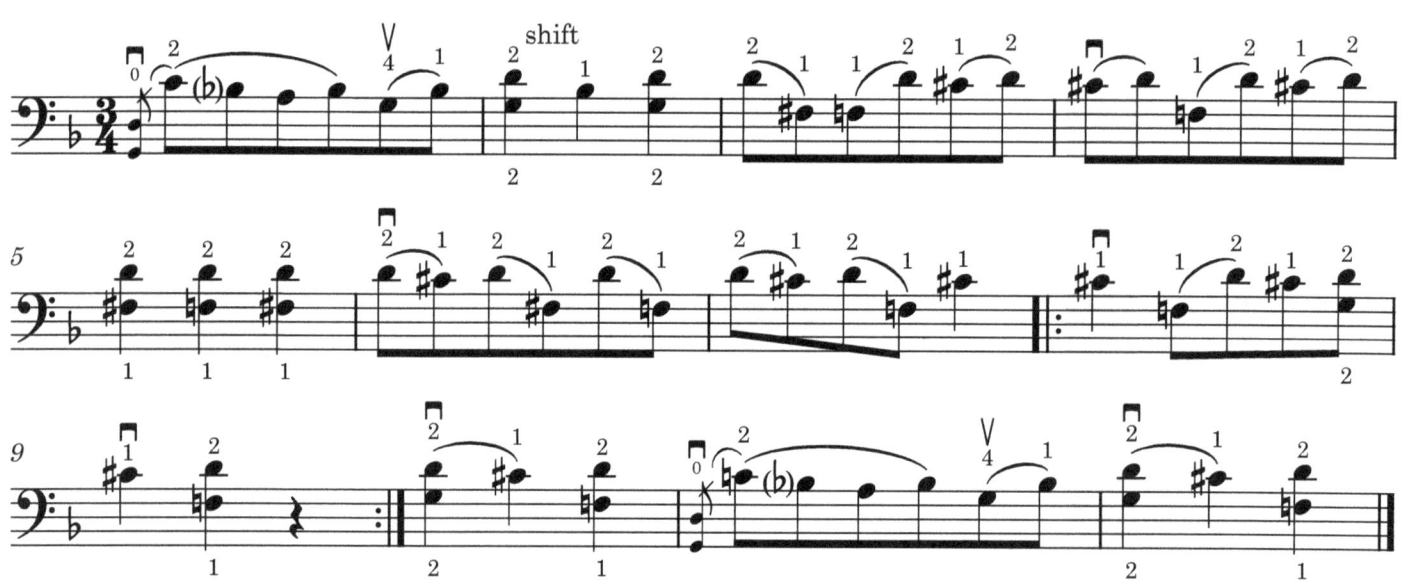

293. Double Stops Across Strings: Measures 21-22

The Bach Cello Suite No. 2 Study Book - Menuet I

294. Shifting to Fourth Position, Top Fingering: Measures 22-23

295. Reaching the Double Stop, Bottom Fingering: Measures 22-23

296. Chords and Trills: Measures 23-24

©2026 C. Harvey Publications® All Rights Reserved.

114 | The Bach Cello Suite No. 2 Study Book - Menuet II

297. *Menuet II, Part One*: Measures 1-8

298. Bowing: Measures 1-8

299. Shifting: Measures 1-3

©2026 C. Harvey Publications® All Rights Reserved.

The Bach Cello Suite No. 2 Study Book - Menuet II

300. Learning the Notes: Measures 3-5

301. Intonation: Measures 1-5

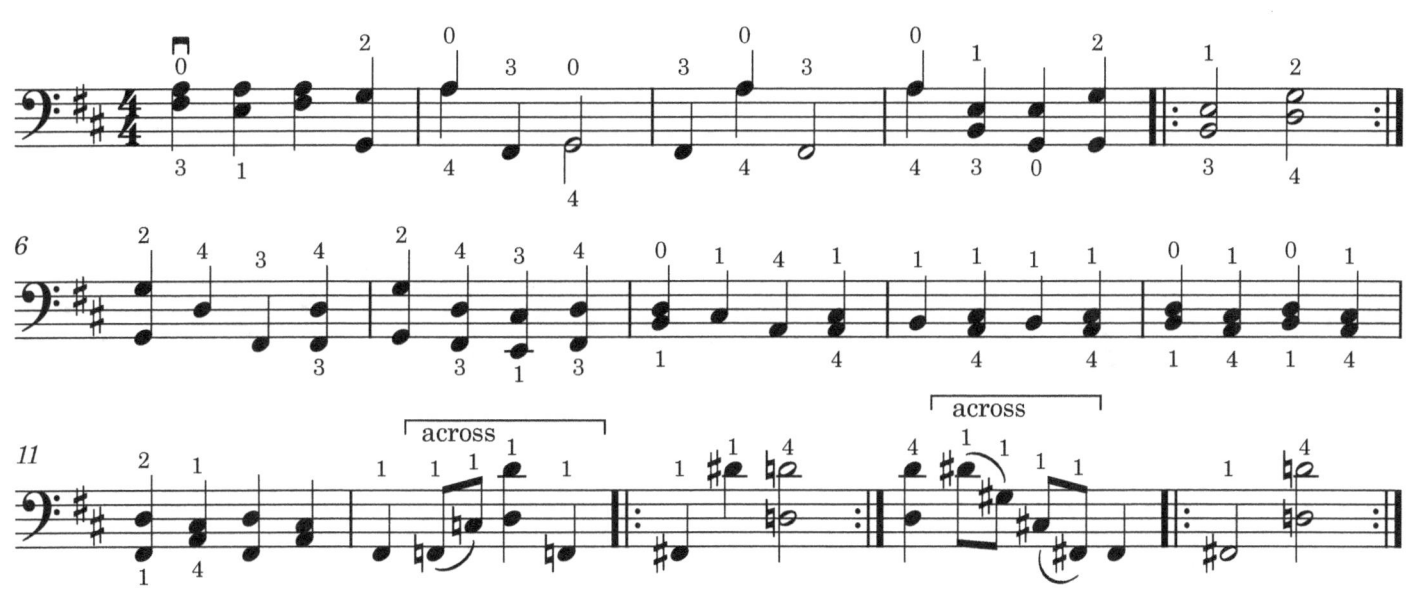

302. Shifting I: Measures 1-5

Repeat each line, playing faster each time.

©2026 C. Harvey Publications® All Rights Reserved.

The Bach Cello Suite No. 2 Study Book - Menuet II

303. Shifting II: Measures 1-5

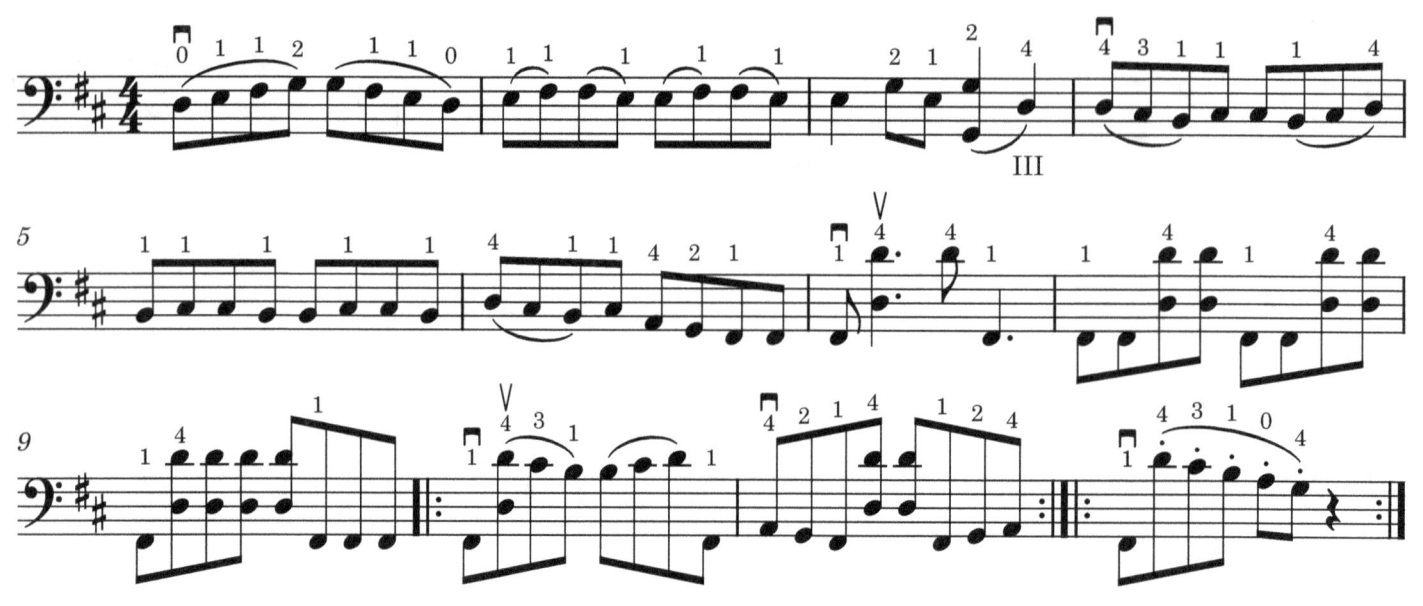

304. Learning the Notes: Measures 6-8

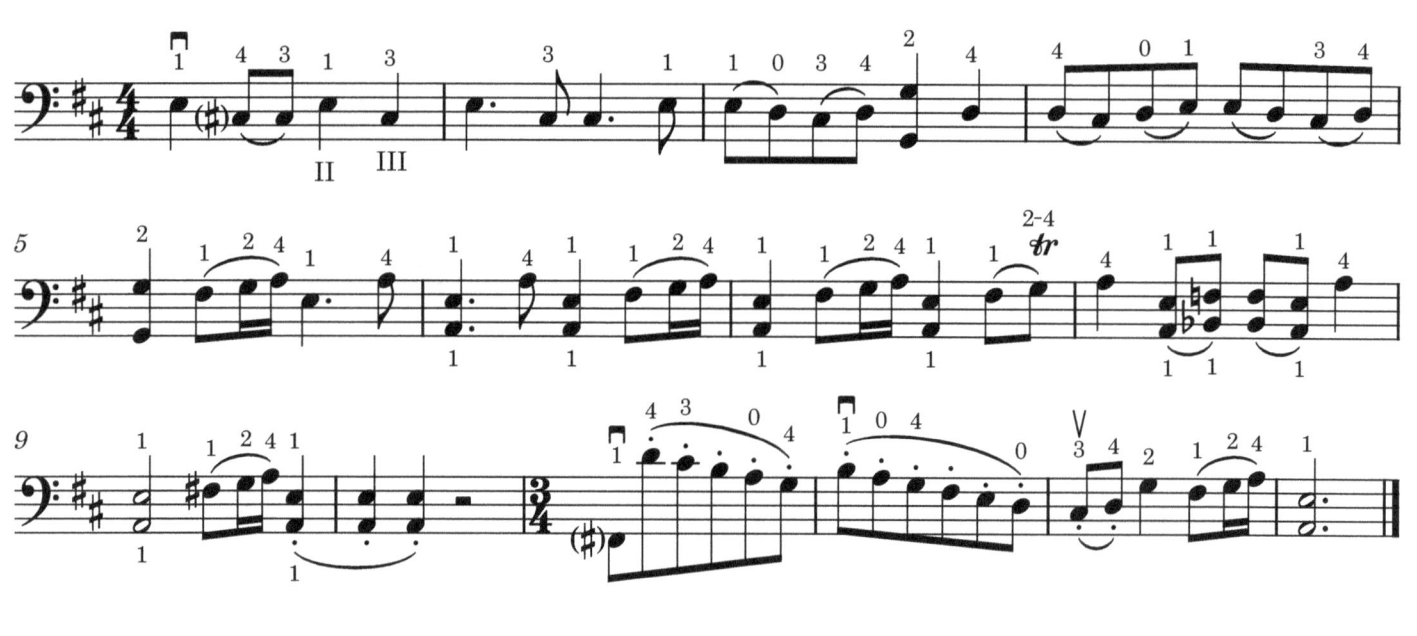

305. *Menuet II, Part Two*: Measures 9-14

♩ = 108–120

The Bach Cello Suite No. 2 Study Book - Menuet II

306. Transitions: Measures 8-9

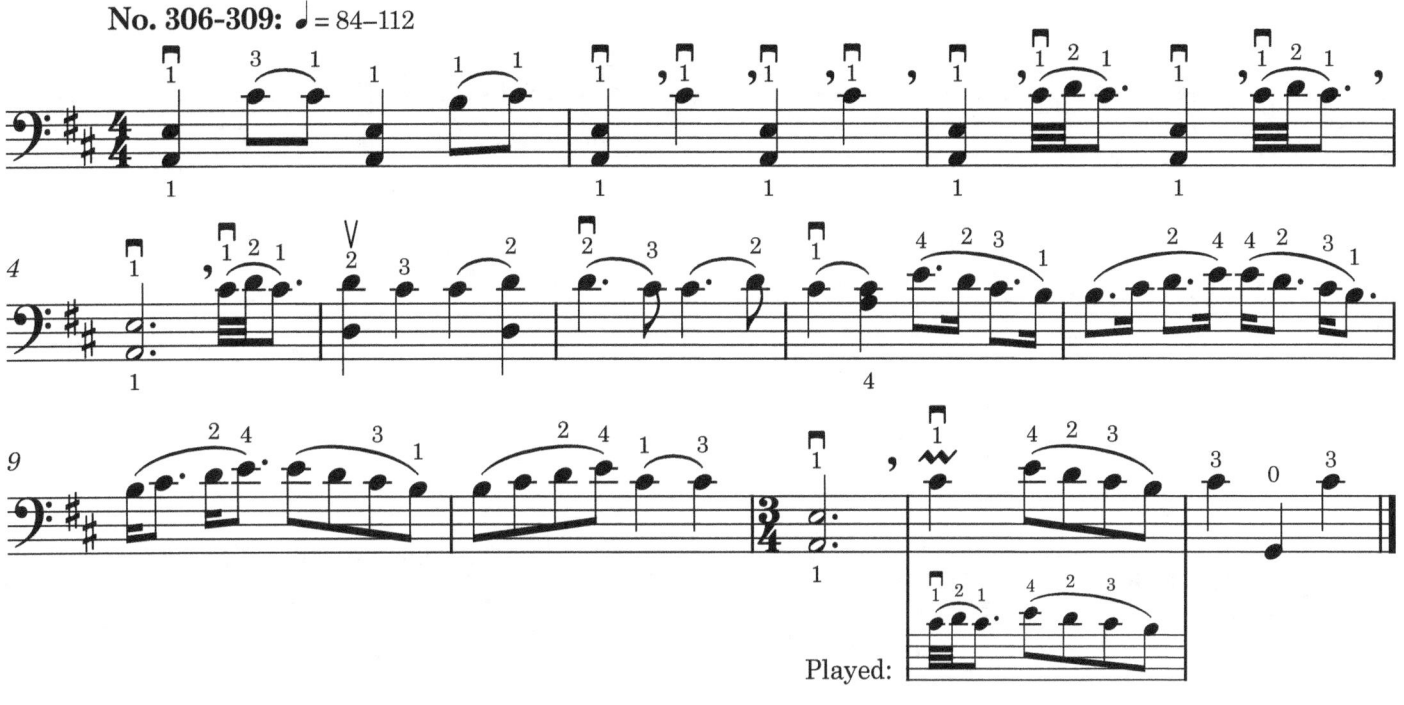

307. Bowing: Measures 8-14

308. Shifting: Measures 11-12

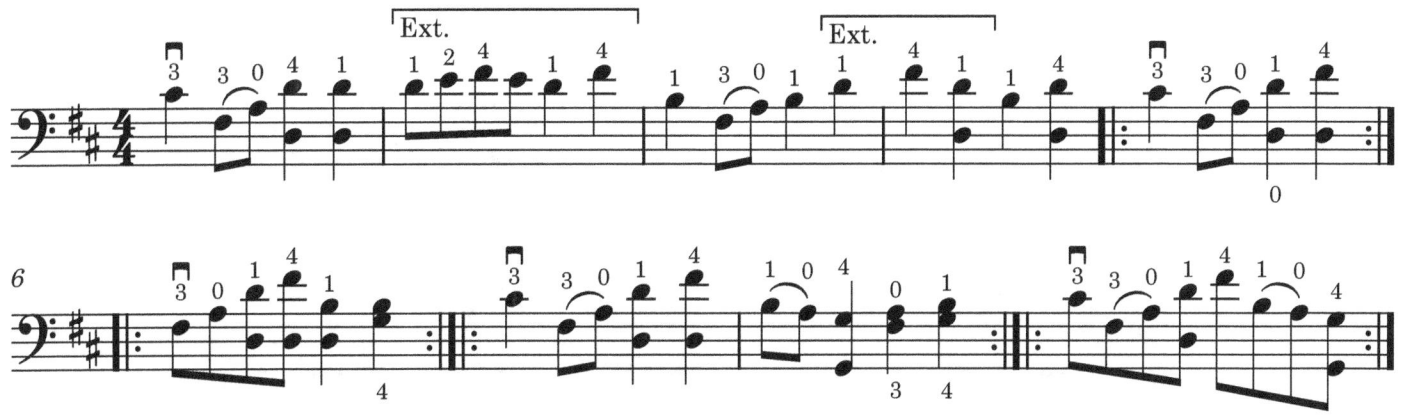

©2026 C. Harvey Publications® All Rights Reserved.

309. Agility: Measures 5-6

310. *Menuet II, Part Three*: Measures 15-24 (end)

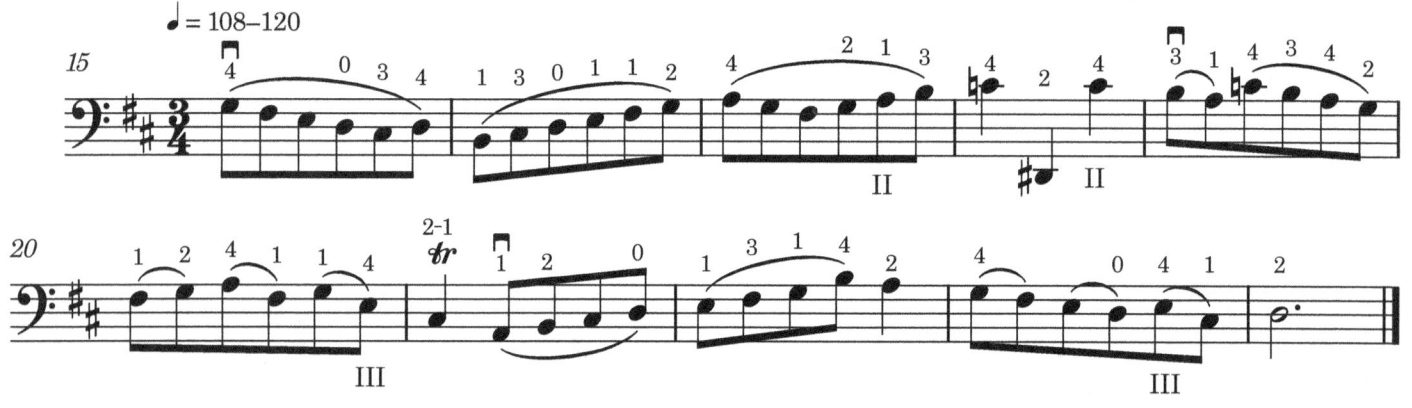

311. Bowing: Measures 15-24

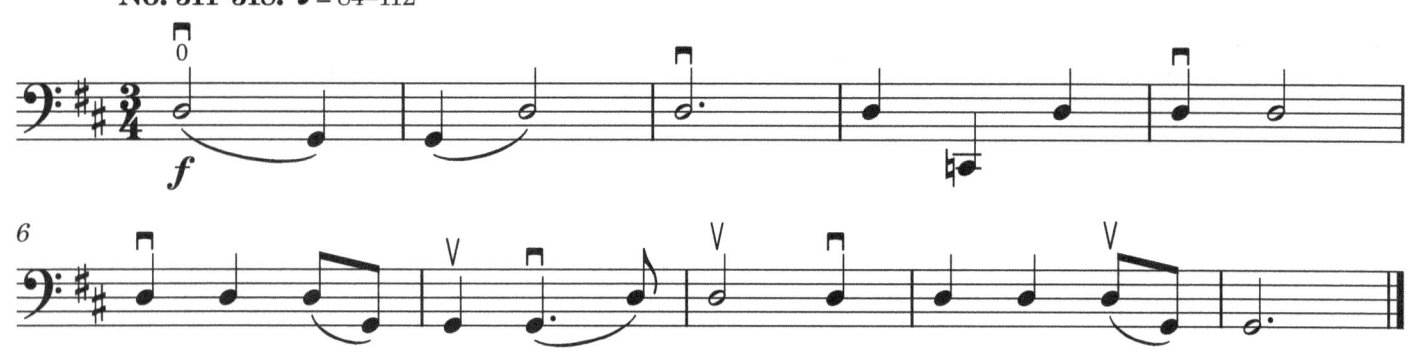

312. Shifting: Measures 15-17

The Bach Cello Suite No. 2 Study Book - Menuet II

313. Intonation and Fluency: Measures 15-17

314. Shifting: Measures 18-19

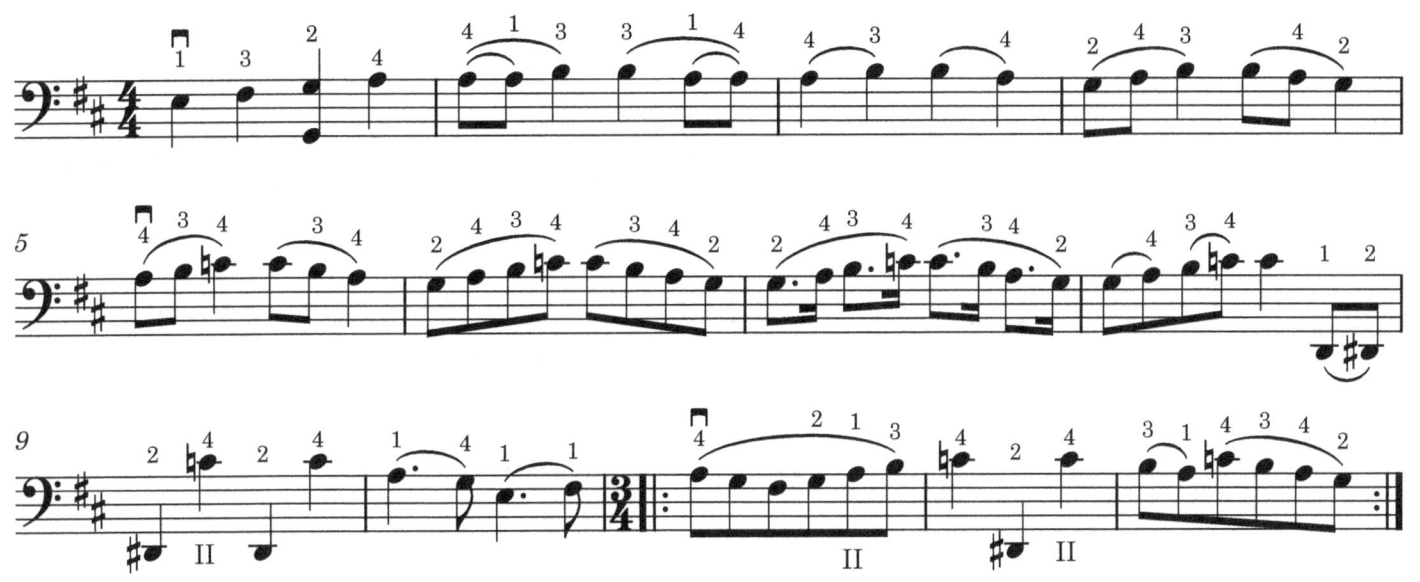

315. Extending Across Strings: Measures 20-21

©2026 C. Harvey Publications® All Rights Reserved.

316. Extending and Shifting: Measures 20-22

317. Shifting: Measures 22-24

The Bach Cello Suite No. 2 Study Book - Gigue 121

321. Shifting: Measure 3

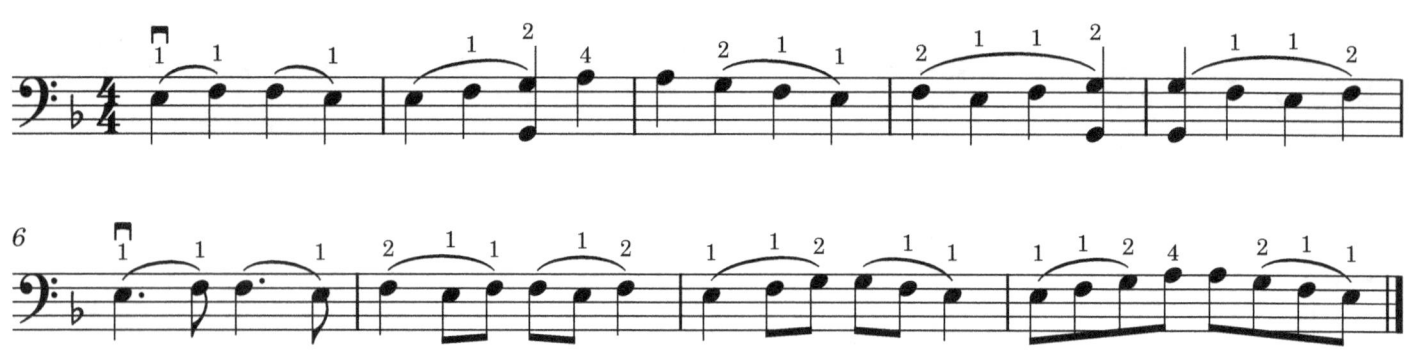

322. Agility and Intonation: Measures 3-5

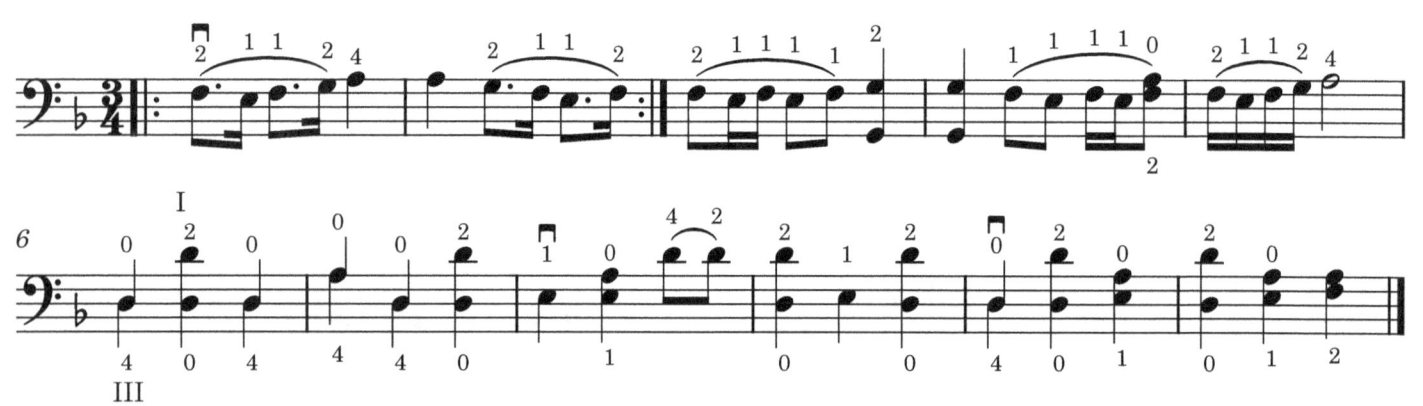

323. Third Position Across Strings: Measures 5-6

The Bach Cello Suite No. 2 Study Book - Gigue

324. Shifting Across Strings: Measure 6

325. Shifting From Fourth to Third Position: Measures 6-7

326. Shifting Backwards to a Trill: Measures 7-8

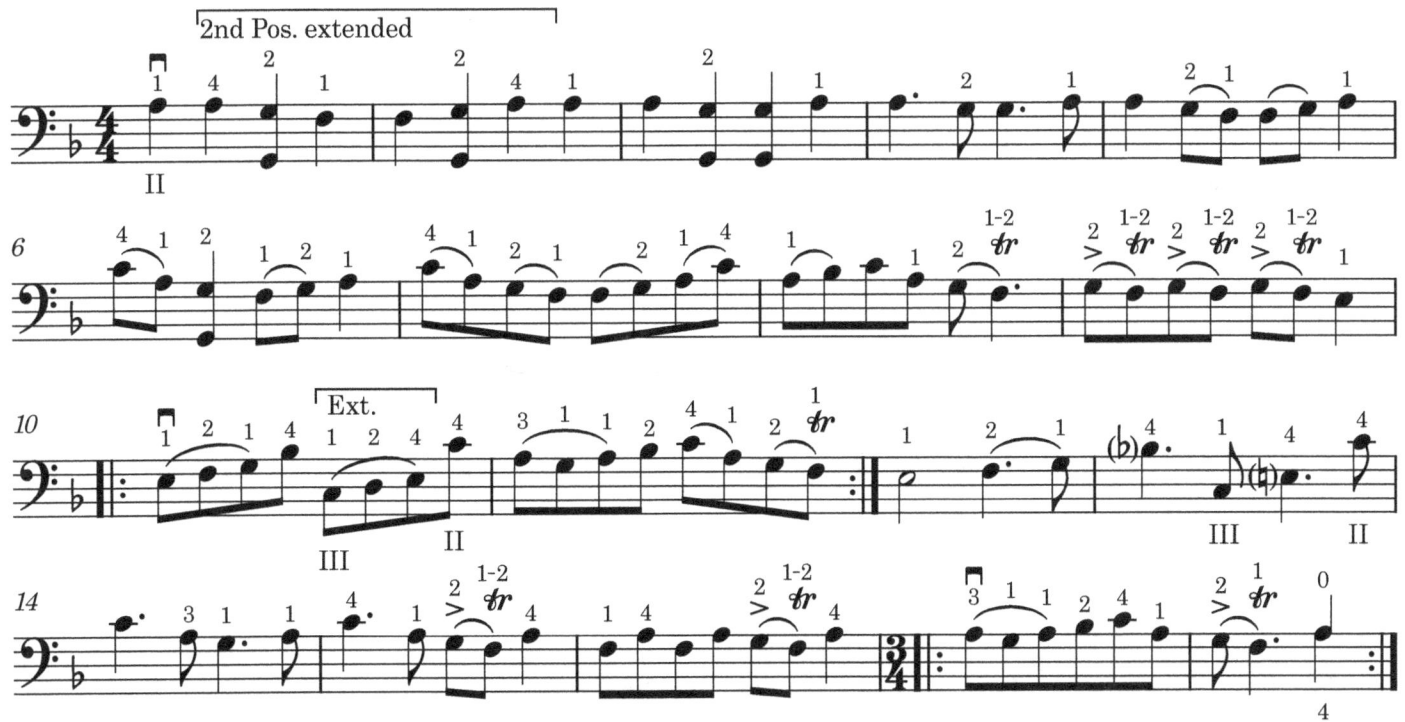

©2026 C. Harvey Publications® All Rights Reserved.

327. *Gigue, Part Two*: Measures 9-14

328. Learning the Notes: Measures 7-10

329. Across Strings in Positions: Measures 11-12

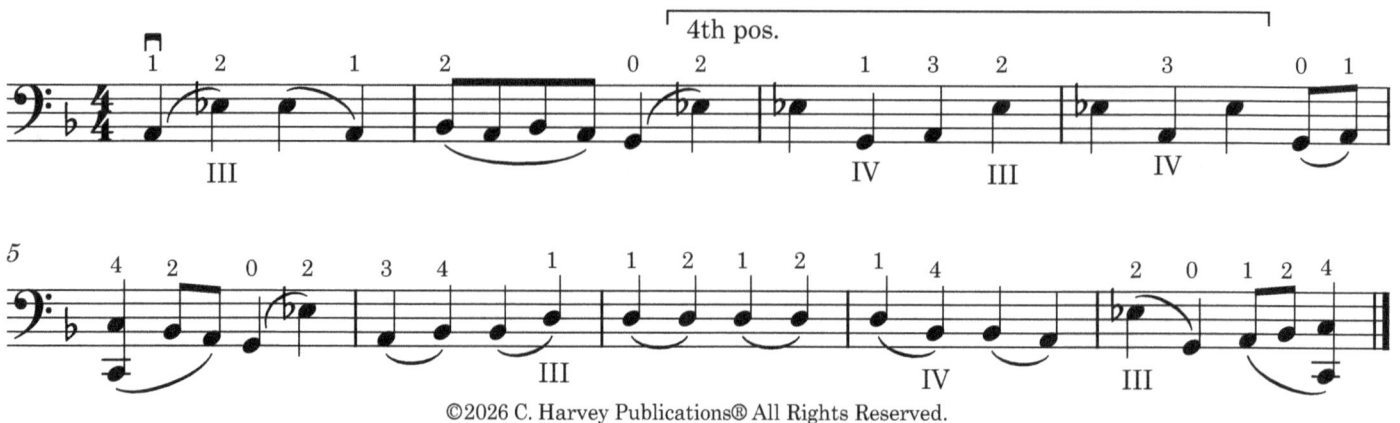

The Bach Cello Suite No. 2 Study Book - Gigue   125

330. Shifting Backwards to Third Position: Measures 11-12

331. Shifting: Measures 12-14

©2026 C. Harvey Publications® All Rights Reserved.

335. How the Measures are Typically Played (Baroque Style): Meas. 15-20

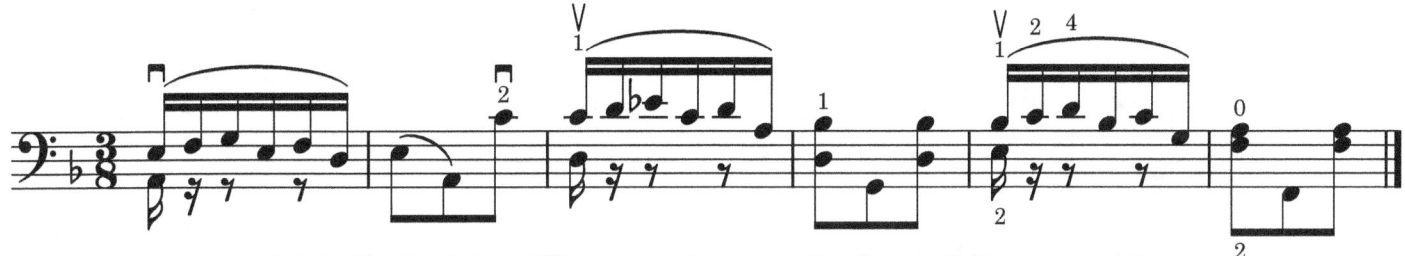

336. Switching Fingers Across Strings: Measure 19

337. Optional Lower, "Literal" Fingering Ex. (Large Hands Only!): Meas. 19

338. Agility: Measures 15-18, *Baroque Style Fingering*

339. Agility: Measures 15-18, *Literal Style Fingering*

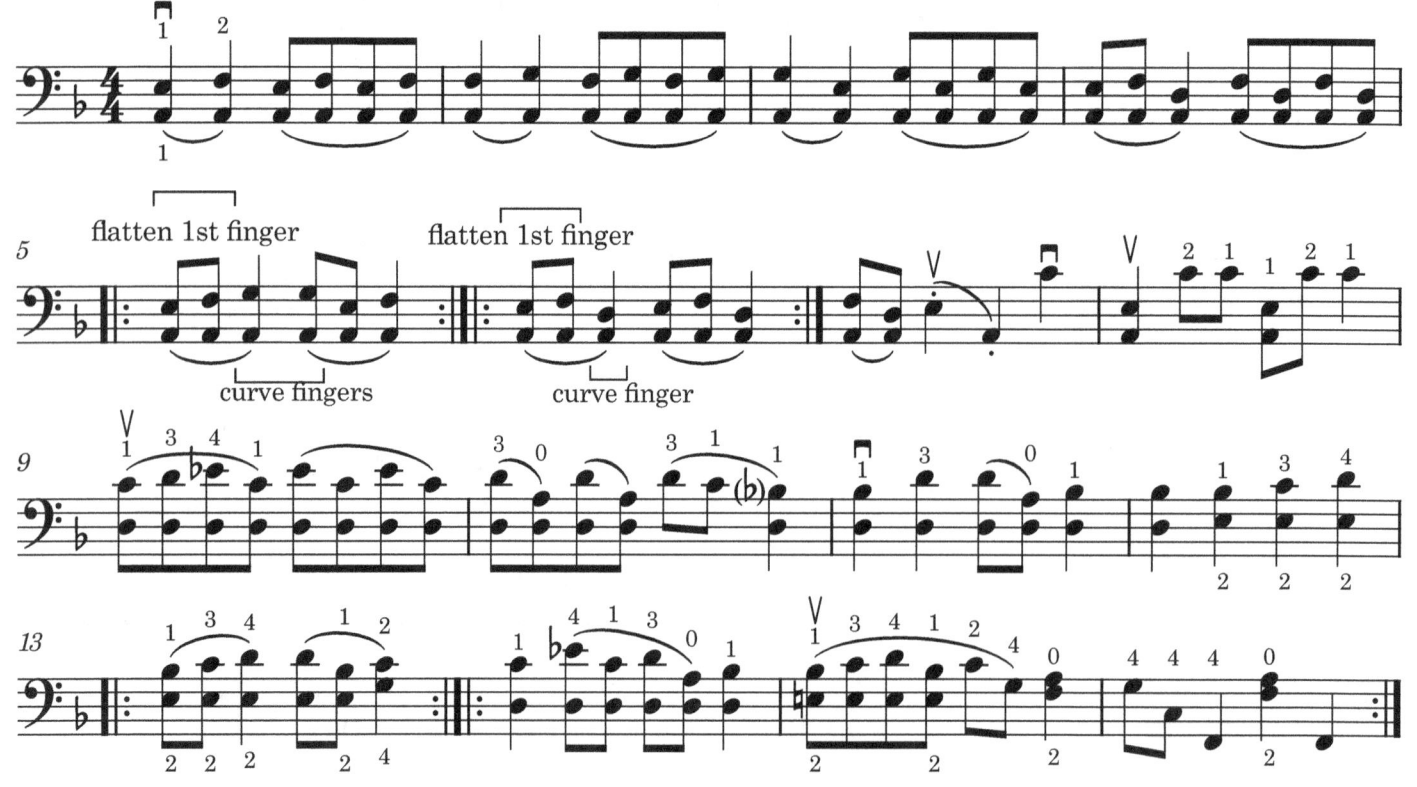

The Bach Cello Suite No. 2 Study Book - Gigue

340. Intonation and Agility: Measures 21-22

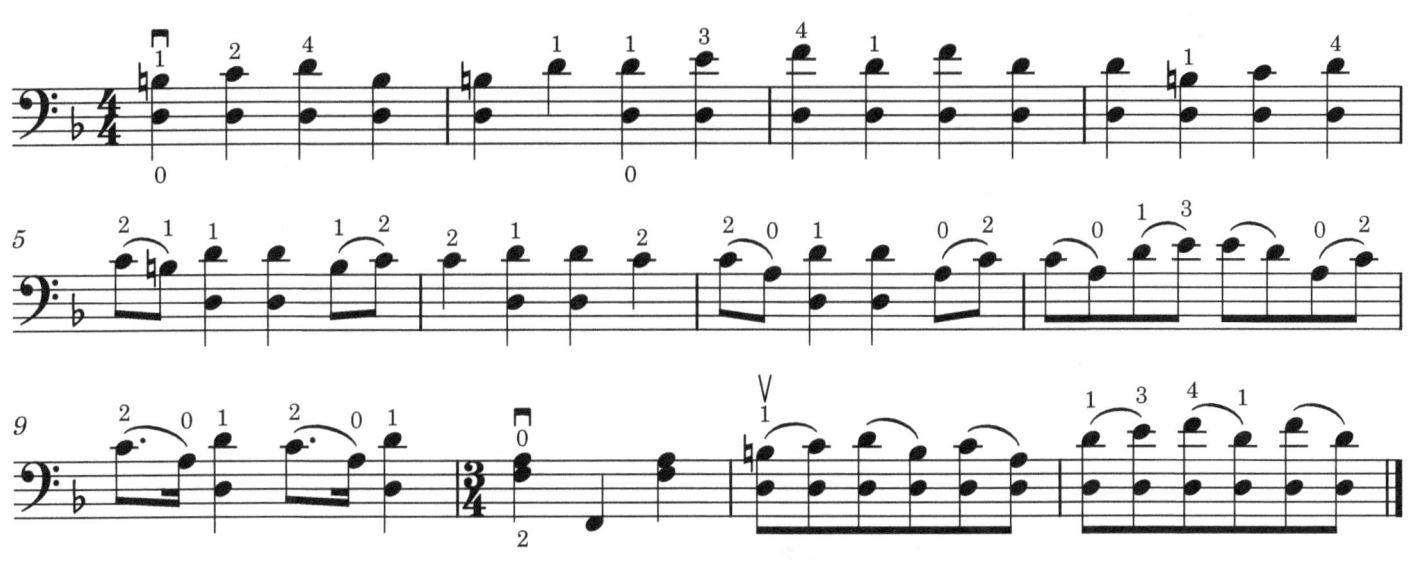

341. Shifting: Measures 22-24

342. *Gigue, Part Four*: Measures 25-32

♩. = 60–72

343. Agility: Measures 25-28

No. 343-347: ♩ = 92–152

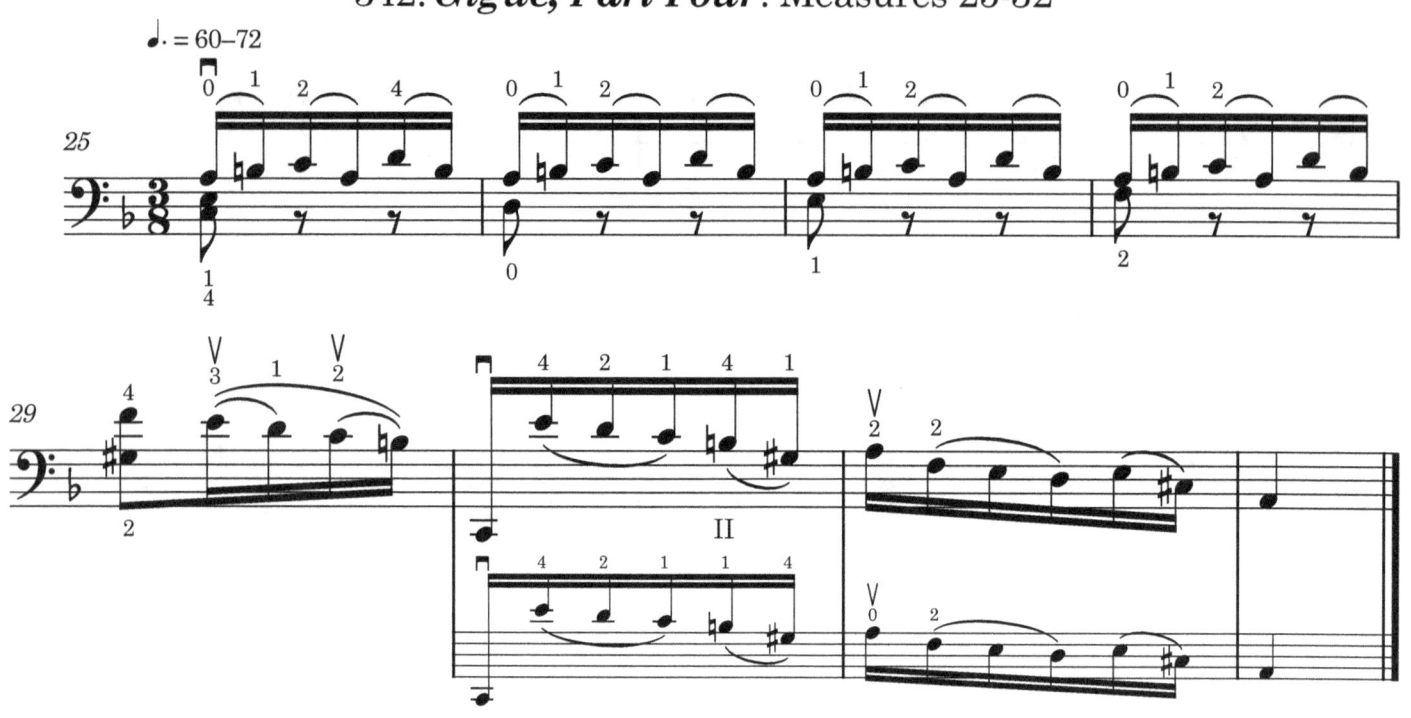

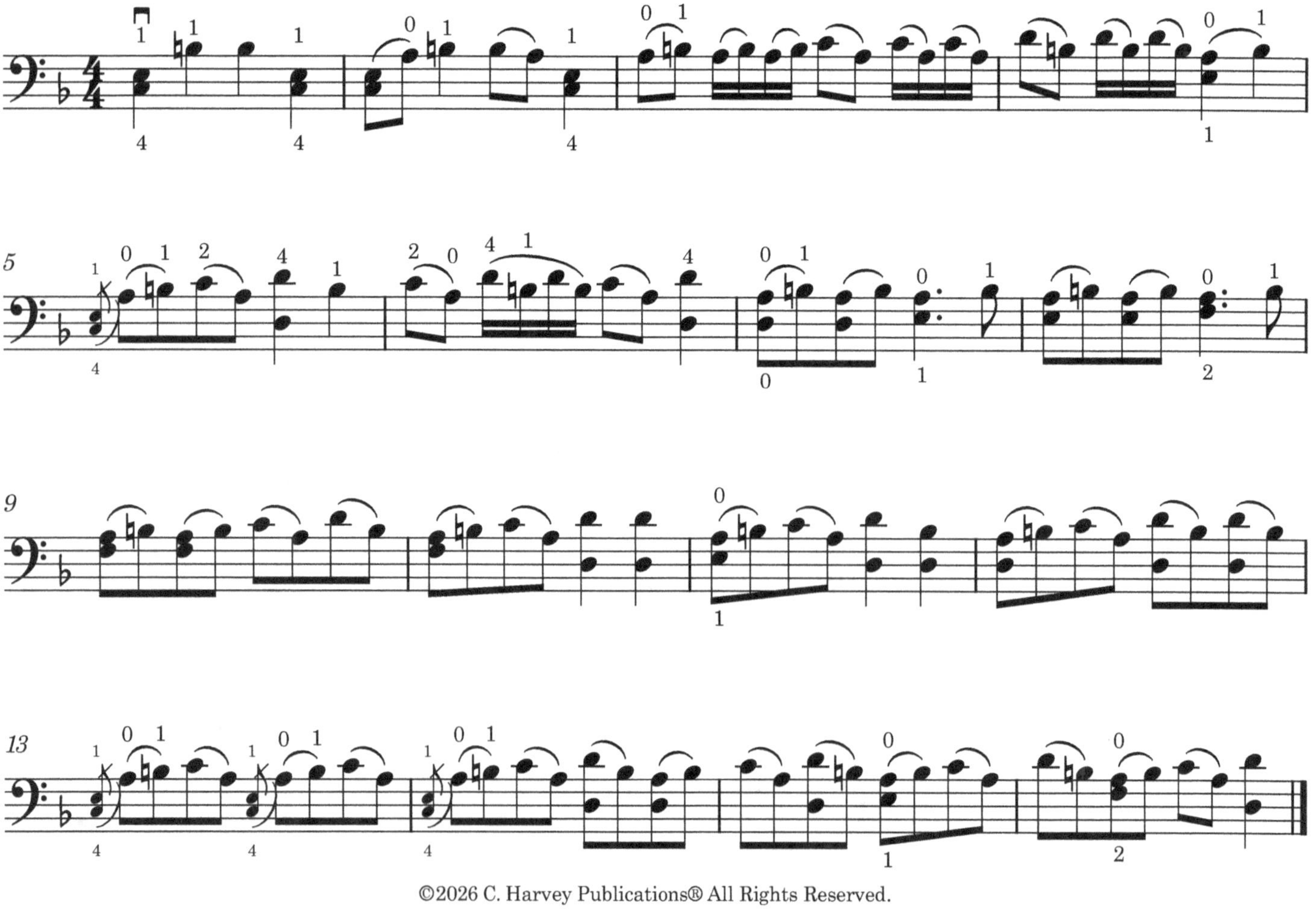

The Bach Cello Suite No. 2 Study Book - Gigue

344. Shifting: Measures 28-29

Simply stop your bow on the string for these repeated up bows or down bows.

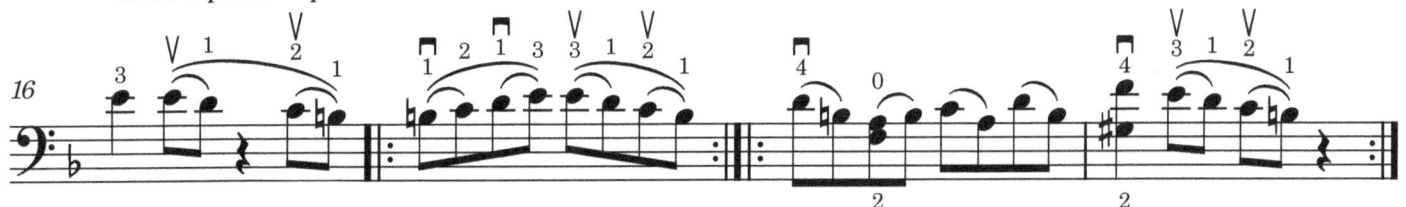

345. Shifting: Measures 29-32

346. Shifting Agility Across Strings: Measures 29-32

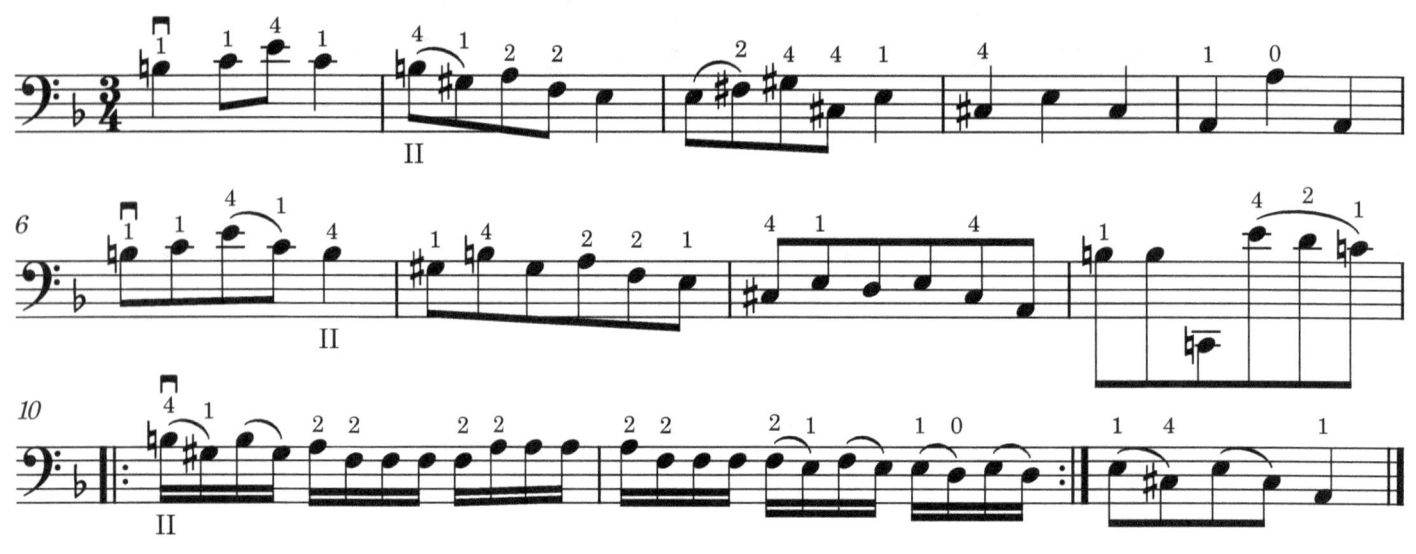

347. Bowing: Measures 25-32

348. *Gigue, Part Five*: Measures 33-40

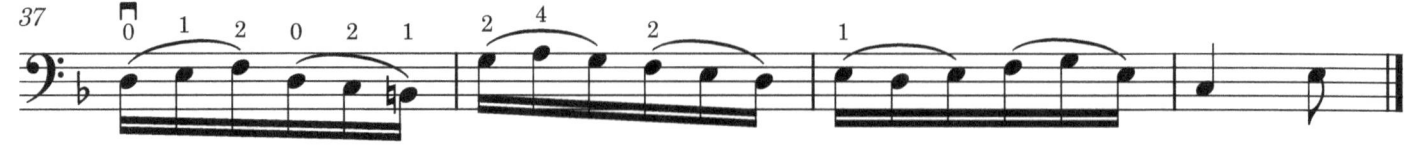

349. Intonation: Measures 33-34

The Bach Cello Suite No. 2 Study Book - Gigue

350. Shifting: Measures 34-36

351. Shifting and Bowing: Measures 37-40

352. *Gigue, Part Six*: Measures 41-48

353. Shifting and Extending in Second Position: Measures 40-42

The Bach Cello Suite No. 2 Study Book - Gigue

354. Shifting and Extending in Third Position: Measures 42-44

355. Shifting Between Third and Second Position: Measures 44-46

356. More Third Position to Second Position: Measures 45-47

The Bach Cello Suite No. 2 Study Book - Gigue   137

357. Closed Third Position to Extended Second Position: Measures 46-47

358. Fluency: Measures 46-48

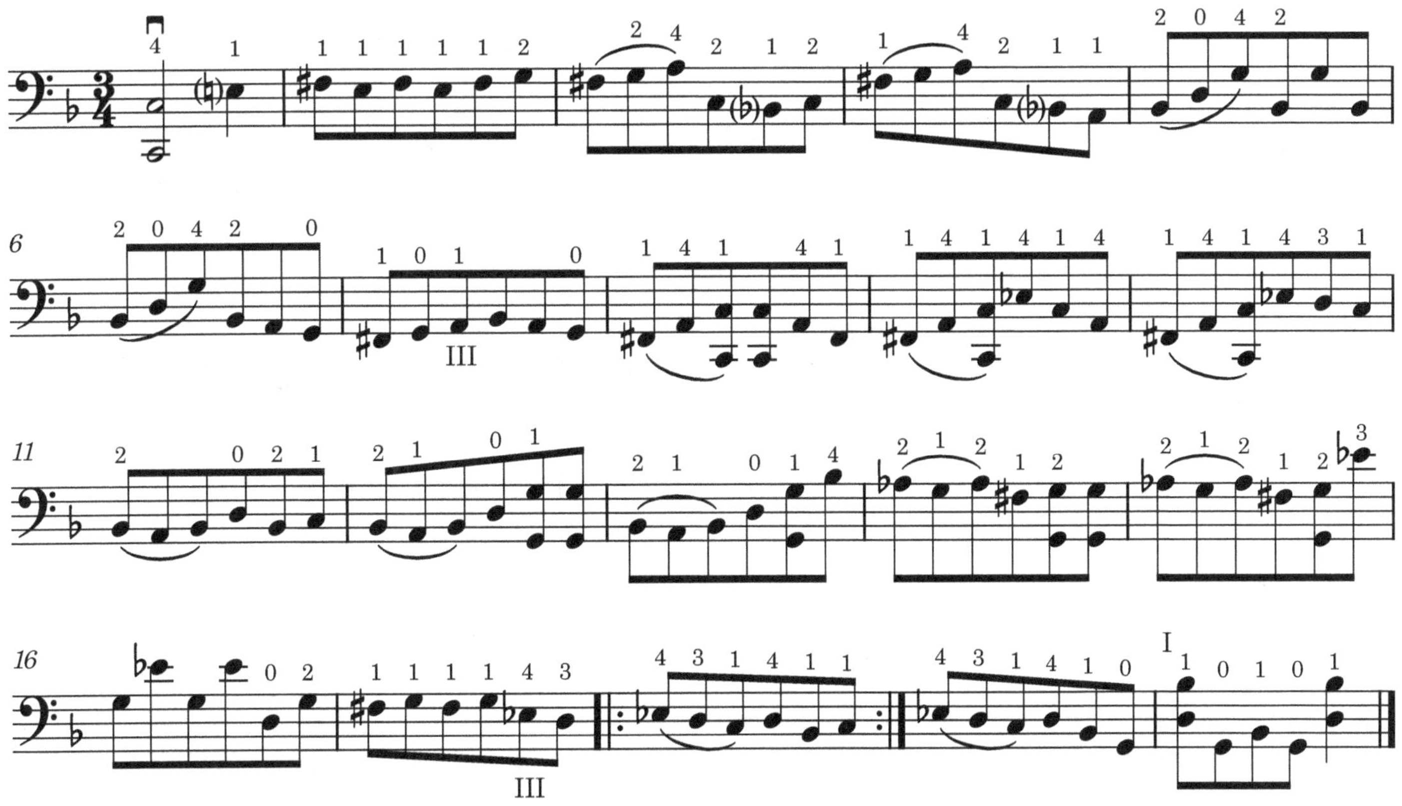

©2026 C. Harvey Publications® All Rights Reserved.

359. *Gigue, Part Seven*: Measures 49-60

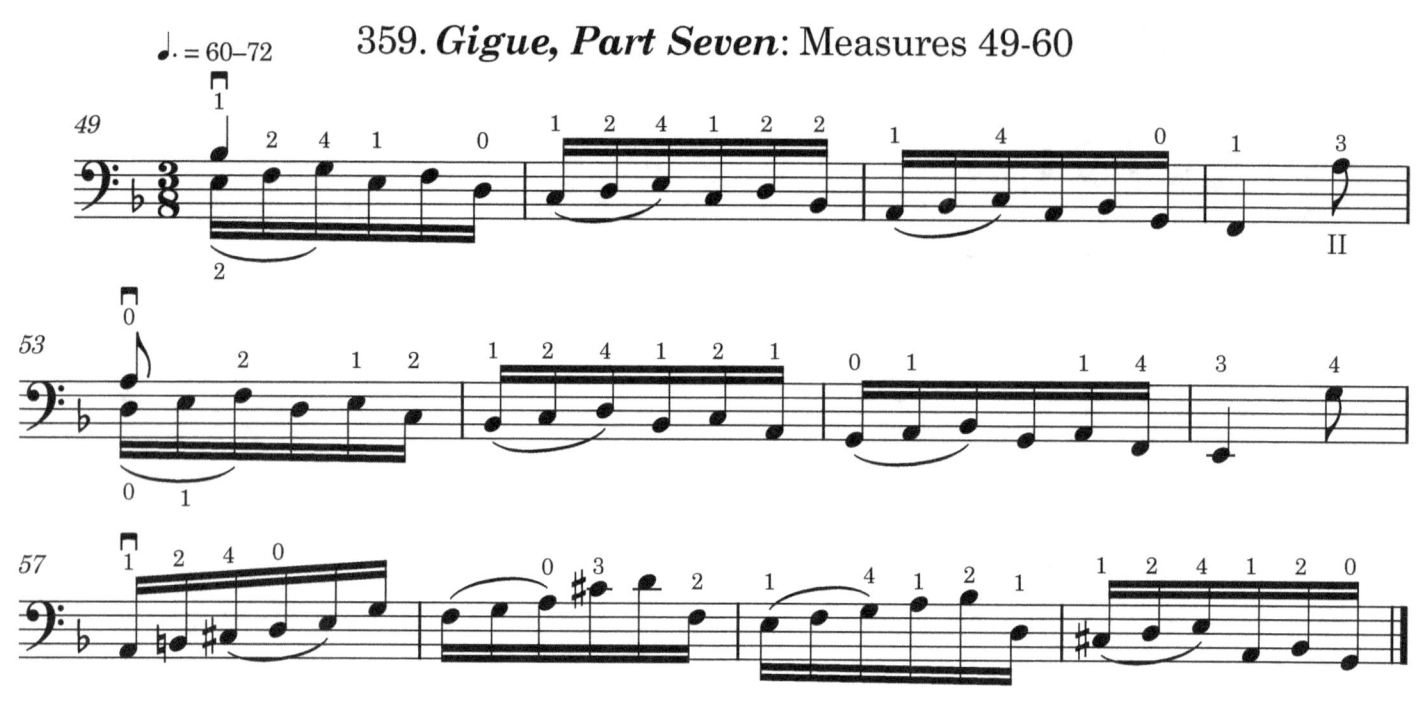

360. Shifting Out of Half Position: Measure 49

361. How the Measure is Typically Played: Measure 49

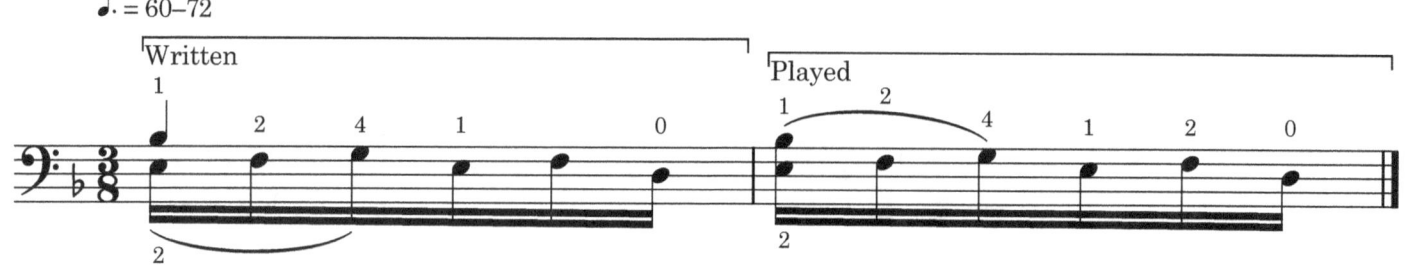

The Bach Cello Suite No. 2 Study Book - Gigue

362. Shifting From an Open String: Measures 50-52

363. Fluency: Measures 49-52

364. Shifting: Measures 52-56

365. Intonation: Measures 56-58

The Bach Cello Suite No. 2 Study Book - Gigue

366. Shifting to Fourth and Third Position: Measures 59-60

367. *Gigue, Part Eight*: Measures 61-76 (end)

The Bach Cello Suite No. 2 Study Book - Gigue

368. Agility: Measures 61-64

No. 368-375: ♩ = 92–152

369. Shifting Across Strings: Measures 64-65

©2026 C. Harvey Publications® All Rights Reserved.

The Bach Cello Suite No. 2 Study Book - Gigue

370. Shifting Across Two Strings: Measures 65-66

371. Shifting to High Third Position: Measures 66-68

372. Bowing: Measures 65-69

373. Contracting the Hand: Measures 69-70

The Bach Cello Suite No. 2 Study Book - Gigue

374. Reaching the Chord: Measures 71-72

375. Intonation and Fluency: Measures 72-76

©2026 C. Harvey Publications® All Rights Reserved.

Prelude

J. S. Bach

The Bach Cello Suite No. 2 Study Book - Prelude 147

Allemande

The Bach Cello Suite No. 2 Study Book - Allemande

Courante

The Bach Cello Suite No. 2 Study Book - Courante 151

Sarabande

The Bach Cello Suite No. 2 Study Book

Menuet I

Menuet II

Menuet I da Capo

Gigue

The Bach Cello Suite No. 2 Study Book - Gigue

Also available from www.charveypublications.com and www.learnstrings.com:
A book that teaches you every measure of Bach's First Cello Suite

The Bach Cello Suite No. 1 Study Book

Note: The Suite is broken up into sections in this study book. The complete Suite is at the back of the book.

Suite No. 1: Prelude
Part One: Measures 1-4 (Bowing #1)

Suite by J. S. Bach
Exercises by Cassia Harvey

Double Stops for Intonation
Measures 1-4

CHP332 - Print from charveypublications.com
CHPD376 - PDF Download from www.learnstrings.com

www.ingramcontent.com/pod-product-compliance
Lightning Source LLC
Chambersburg PA
CBHW081414080526
44589CB00016B/2529